THE ICE STORM

THE ICE STORM

An historic record in photographs of January 1998, with a text by Mark Abley

M&S

Canadian Cataloguing in Publication Data

Abley, Mark, 1955-
    The ice storm: an historic record in photographs of January 1998

ISBN 0-7710-6100-5

1. Ice storms – Canada, Eastern. 2. Ice storms – Canada, Eastern – Pictorial works. 3. Ice storms – New England. 4. Ice storms – New England – Pictorial works. 5. Ice storms – New York (State). 6. Ice storms – New York (State) – Pictorial works. I. Title.

QC926.45.C2A24 1998   363.34'92   C98-932076-6

Design by Sari Ginsberg
Typesetting by M & S, Toronto
Printed and Bound in Canada by Friesens

McClelland & Stewart acknowledge the financial support of the Government of Canada through the Book Publishing Industry Development Program for our publishing activities. We further acknowl-edge the support of The Canada Council for the Arts and the Ontario Arts Council for our publishing program.

McClelland & Stewart Inc.
The Canadian Publishers
481 University Avenue
Toronto, Ontario
M5G 2E9

Photographs
Front cover: Peter Martin, The Gazette, *Oxford Ave., Notre-Dame-de-Grâce, Montreal.*
Back cover: Dave Sidaway, The Gazette, *Icy window, Saint-Jean-Baptiste-de-Rouville, Quebec*; Bruno Schlumberger, Ottawa Citizen, *Gerald Myles with candle, Ramsay Township, Ontario*; Robert Skinner, La Presse, *Fallen pylon, South Shore, Montreal.*
End papers and opposite page: André Pichette, The Gazette, *Trees, Mount Royal.*

Mount Royal in the freezing rain. (André Pichette, The Gazette)

Icy twig. (Phil Kall, Brockville Recorder and Times)

Table of Contents

Foreword

This book about the January 1998 ice storm which crippled significant parts of eastern Canada and the northeastern United States is the result of a unique collaboration among nine newspapers.

It is the public's expectation that in times of crisis local newspapers will rise to the occasion, and during the ice storm these nine newspapers played a critical role in keeping our readers informed about what was happening in our communities.

Newspapers are accustomed to covering crises but the ice storm was unique because many of our journalists and photographers were confronting the problems caused by living without heat and electricity in their own homes while covering the storm and its aftermath.

When it seemed that everything else had come to a standstill, the newspapers were still being published. In many cases the mail was not delivered but the newspaper carriers somehow managed to get their papers to their subscribers' doors.

The silver lining in the dark days of the ice storm was that we discovered that we can depend on one another. It was that same spirit of cooperation which led us to join together to publish this book documenting a period which, for those who lived through it, will not be forgotten.

We hope that this record in words and photographs of the ice storm will serve as an evocative reminder of the remarkable days we lived through in January 1998.

- Pierre Bergeron, Publisher, Le Droit (Ottawa)

- John Farrington, Publisher, The Cornwall Standard Freeholder

- Pierre Gobeil, Publisher, La Voix de l'Est (Granby)

- Michael Goldbloom, President and Publisher, The Gazette (Montreal)

- Hunter S. Grant, President and Co-Publisher, The Brockville Recorder and Times

- Fred Laflamme, Publisher, The Kingston Whig-Standard

- Roger D. Landry, President and Publisher, La Presse (Montreal)

- Russell A. Mills, President and Publisher, The Ottawa Citizen

- Jean Sisto, President and Publisher, Le Nouvelliste (Trois-Rivières)

Acknowledgements

For everyone touched by the ice storm and its aftermath, as for the journalists and newspaper photographers who covered the ordeal, it was a once-in-a-lifetime story. The ice storm of January 1998 was the most destructive weather disaster in Canada's recorded history. Millions of homes and businesses were blacked out. In Quebec, some were without power for up to 33 days. Some people died as a result of the storm. Many more were left vulnerable, isolated and afraid. The extent of the damage was staggering and it will take years for the landscape to recover.

But this was more than a weather and hydro crisis. It was also a story about people and their heroic fight to restore power and prevent loss of life.

There were many heroes. In the thousands, soldiers, hydro workers from across the country, emergency workers, volunteers and ordinary citizens battled the elements to help each other, to keep each other safe and to get life back to normal.

The storm and its aftermath reminded us of some immutable truths — of our fragility, of nature's strength and of our remarkable ability to pull together in times of need.

In this book, we have tried to tell that story in more than 200 photographs taken by the best of Canada's news photographers and in a text by Mark Abley of The Gazette.

Many other talented people contributed to this book. The Gazette's Alison Marks has been instrumental in making this project possible. Special thanks go to Jean Goupil of La Presse, Alain Dion and Michel St-Jean of La Voix de l'Est, Doris Dionne of Le Nouvelliste, Dave Taylor of The Brockville Recorder and Times, Ian MacAlpine of The Kingston Whig-Standard, and to Drew Gragg, Scott Parker, Wayne Cuddington and Claire Gigantes of The Ottawa Citizen. I would also like to thank The Gazette's Dennis Dubinsky, Armand Favreau, Arden Lanthier, Tim Simpson and Robert Ramsey.

Very special thanks to Charly Bouchara for his excellent work on the French-language version of the book, and to Hélène Lecaudey.

Jennifer Robinson
Editor
Jennifer Robinson is Associate Editor of Montreal's The Gazette.

Left: Storm devastation in Hemmingford, Quebec. (John Kenney, The Gazette)

Introduction

It was the ice storm of the century, five days of freezing rain that caused chaos and destruction, darkness and death. Day after day, its grip on eastern Canada and the northeastern United States tightened. Steel towers, hydro poles and trees collapsed under the weight of the ice. Millions of people were blacked out for days or weeks, many forced into shelters, many others left in the cold and dark, isolated and vulnerable.

Homes, farms and businesses in eastern Ontario, southwestern Quebec, northeastern United States and the Maritime provinces were without power for days or even weeks on end as the temperature fluctuated between mild and extreme. In some parts, business ground to a halt.

In the hardest-hit region known as the "triangle of darkness" in Quebec, where Environment Canada estimates that 100 millimetres (roughly four inches) of freezing rain fell, the hydro-electric system was destroyed. The rest of Hydro-Quebec's power grid was holding by a fragile thread.

The highest amount of freezing rain – 78.4 millimetres – was recorded by Environment Canada at Saint-Hubert, Quebec. In the "triangle of darkness" that included Saint-Hyacinthe, Farnham and Saint-Jean-sur-Richelieu, where there are no weather stations, Environment Canada believes that up to 100 millimetres of freezing rain may have fallen. (Michel St-Jean, La Voix de l'Est)

Left: Gunner Patrick Szilbereisz and his Canadian Forces contingent help Hydro-Quebec clear downed wires just west of Saint-Jean-sur-Richelieu. Including reservists, about 16,000 troops – roughly 12,000 in Quebec and 4,000 in Ontario – worked to clear fallen trees, limbs and hydro wires, move citizens to shelters and maintain civil order. It was the largest humanitarian assistance mobilization of the Canadian Forces in history. (Gordon Beck, The Gazette)

A line of fallen pylons. (Bernard Brault, La Presse)

Montreal was on the verge of disaster, its entire downtown core and west end in the dark. The army and police patrolled the streets.

The storm and its aftermath brought out the best and the worst in those it touched. Courage. Ingenuity and patience. Fear and anxiety. Greed. Compassion and a sense of community. A willingness to help those in need.

THE BLACKOUTS

More than 5 million people were affected by at least one power outage.

• In Quebec, 1.4 million customers, representing an estimated 3.5 million people, or half the population, were blacked out. The longest residential blackouts lasted 33 days.

• In Ontario, 235,000 customers, or about 600,000 people, lost power.

• In New Brunswick, 28,000 customers were without power.

• In Nova Scotia, 20,000 customers lost power.

• More than 545,000 customers, representing well over a million people, were blacked out in the United States because of the storm. In Maine, where 315,000 customers lost power, a general state of emergency was declared. In New Hampshire, 67,000 customers were without power and a state of emergency was declared in nine of 10 counties. In New York, 130,000 customers lost power and a state of emergency was declared in 10 of 62 counties. In Vermont, where 33,000 customers lost power, a state of emergency was declared in six of 14 counties.

HYDRO

• In Quebec, more than 3,000 kilometres of Hydro-Quebec's power network broke down. In all, 24,000 poles, 4,000 transformers and 1,000 steel pylons were damaged. The cost of repairs will exceed $800 million.

• In Ontario, an estimated 11,000 poles, 1,000 transformers and 300 steel towers were damaged.

THE FARMS

Livestock, poultry, maple groves, apple orchards and forests all suffered in the storm and the blackout. Without power, more than 5,000 dairy farmers reportedly had to dump 13.5 million litres of milk worth an estimated $7.8 million.

• In Quebec, 17,000 farms were affected by the storm. Preliminary estimates show losses worth $14 million.

• In eastern Ontario, 10,000 farms were affected. Losses are estimated at $11 million.

THE TREES

Millions of trees were damaged or destroyed by the weight of the ice, and there is no way to measure the extent of the damage to the region. On Montreal's Mount Royal alone, at least 140,000 trees were damaged, roughly 80 per cent of the trees on the mountain, and 5,000 were completely destroyed. The cost of the clean-up, pruning and replacement on the mountain is estimated at $15 million.

THE DAMAGE

The Insurance Bureau of Canada estimates that final insurance claims for damage caused by the ice storm will exceed $1.1 billion. By mid-1998,

• 576,950 claims had been filed in Quebec, valued at $871 million;

• 77,000 claims had been filed in Ontario, valued at $200 million; and

• 200 claims had been filed in Atlantic Canada, valued at $2 million.

January 12, Main Street, Granby. (Alain Dion, La Voix de l'Est)

Ernest and Ethel Jubien, shown here in 1991 in the rose garden at their Town of Mount Royal home, were among 22 Quebecers who died in the ice storm and its aftermath. Their home was set ablaze as they tried to keep warm in front of a fireplace during the blackout. Four people died in storm-related incidents in Ontario. Six people died in New York and three in Maine. Fire, hypothermia, carbon monoxide poisoning and falling ice were the main causes. (Marie-France Coallier, The Gazette)

• The short-term economic costs of the storm have been estimated at $1.4 billion in Quebec and $200 million in Ontario.

THE HELP

There was no shortage of generosity and compassion during the storm and the blackout. Police, firefighters, soldiers, medical workers, volunteers, neighbours, family and friends pulled together to help and console, to keep each other safe.

• In Quebec, 454 shelters were set up to house people who had lost power and could not heat their homes. In Ontario, 85 shelters were established. Thousands of volunteers made it possible.

• Health Canada supplied 24,000 cots, 76,000 blankets, and 8,840 stretchers to shelters.

• The Canadian Red Cross reports that $11.5 million was donated for ice-storm relief. During the storm and its aftermath, 3,300 staff and volunteers helped more than 334,000 people.

• About 16,000 military troops and reservists were called in, 12,000 in Quebec and 4,000 in Ontario. They often received a hero's welcome.

THE DEATHS

In all, 35 people died from storm-related causes such as house fires, falling ice, carbon monoxide poisoning and hypothermia. In Quebec, 22 people died. Four died in Ontario, six in New York and three in Maine.

The road to Farnham. (Michel St-Jean, La Voix de l'Est)

Above: Gary and Jacqueline Stewart look around their fire-damaged home in Russell, Ontario. (John Major, Ottawa Citizen)

Right: People used generators, fireplaces, gas stoves and even candles to try to heat their homes during the blackout, often with disastrous results. This photo shows firemen trying to put out a blaze on January 7 at Ottawa Citizen editor Neil Reynolds's home in Rockcliffe, Ontario. (Patrick Doyle, Ottawa Citizen)

Above: Dairy farmers need electricity to operate wells, heat barns, and help in feeding and milking their cows. During the blackout, many cattle died. In this picture, Ginette Hebert, office manager of Machabee Animal Food Ltd. in St. Albert, Ontario, walks past a pile of dead Holsteins that perished from storm-related causes. (Dave Chan, Ottawa Citizen)

Top left: Icicles. (Todd Lihou, Cornwall Standard Freeholder)

Bottom left: This building on LaSalle Boulevard in Verdun collapsed under the weight of the ice on its roof. (John Kenney, The Gazette)

Left: Railroad crossing on Route 235 near Farnham.
(Michel St-Jean, La Voix de l'Est)

Right: Nearly a month after the freezing rain, dead wood was piled high on Mount Royal as the clean-up began. Four out of five trees on the mountain were damaged in the storm and 5,000 were destroyed. (Armand Trottier, La Presse)

Inside the ice storm: how freezing rain forms

Freezing rain, like the inundation that took place for five days starting January 5, 1998 occurs close to the junction of a warm moving air mass and a stationary cold air mass. It's the layering of warm air over cold, as one air mass glides over another, that allows freezing rain and ice pellets to form.

It's only within a fairly narrow belt close to the junction of the air masses that conditions are right for freezing rain. And that zone is precisely where the Montreal region and eastern Ontario found themselves in early January.

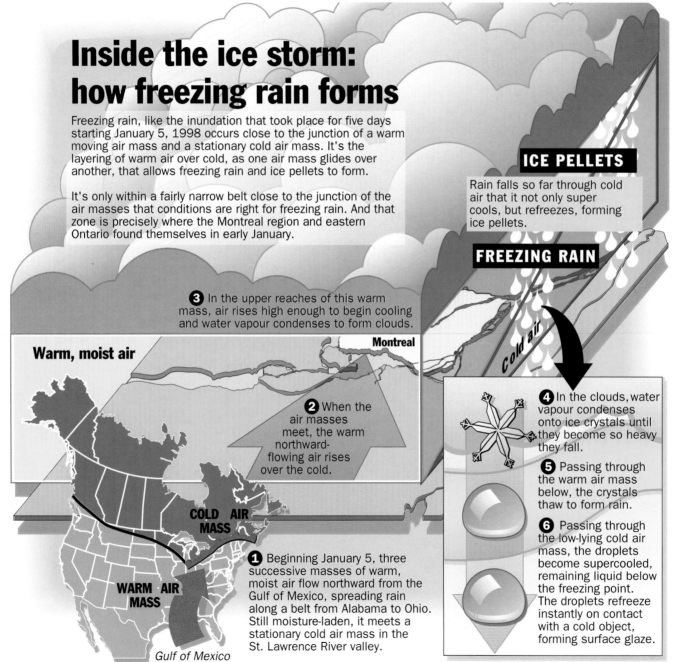

ICE PELLETS

Rain falls so far through cold air that it not only super cools, but refreezes, forming ice pellets.

FREEZING RAIN

Cold air

3 In the upper reaches of this warm mass, air rises high enough to begin cooling and water vapour condenses to form clouds.

Warm, moist air

Montreal

2 When the air masses meet, the warm northward-flowing air rises over the cold.

COLD AIR MASS

WARM AIR MASS

Gulf of Mexico

1 Beginning January 5, three successive masses of warm, moist air flow northward from the Gulf of Mexico, spreading rain along a belt from Alabama to Ohio. Still moisture-laden, it meets a stationary cold air mass in the St. Lawrence River valley.

4 In the clouds, water vapour condenses onto ice crystals until they become so heavy they fall.

5 Passing through the warm air mass below, the crystals thaw to form rain.

6 Passing through the low-lying cold air mass, the droplets become supercooled, remaining liquid below the freezing point. The droplets refreeze instantly on contact with a cold object, forming surface glaze.

Dean Tweed, Gazette

Above: At the outset, road crews salted and tried to clear roads as the freezing rain came down. (Sylvain Marier, Le Droit)

Right: Rain, hail and snow might not stop the mail, but the ice storm did on Route 235 near Farnham. (Michel St-Jean, La Voix de l'Est)

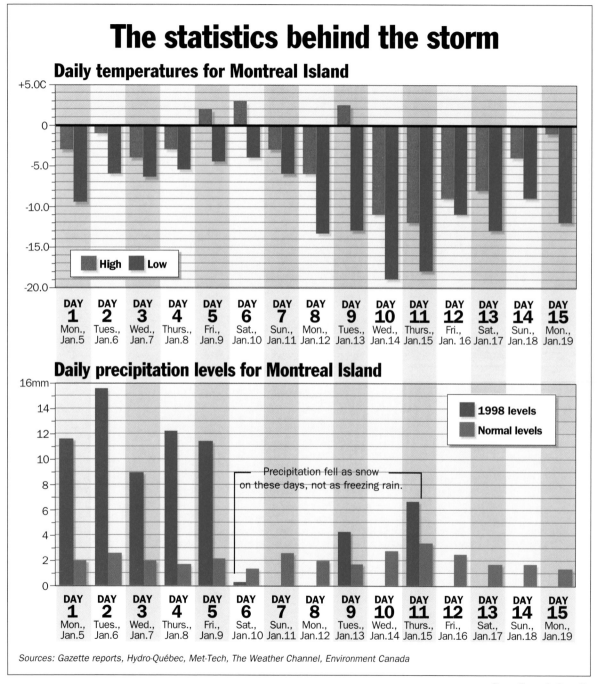

The statistics behind the storm

Daily temperatures for Montreal Island

Legend: High, Low

| | DAY 1 Mon., Jan.5 | DAY 2 Tues., Jan.6 | DAY 3 Wed., Jan.7 | DAY 4 Thurs., Jan.8 | DAY 5 Fri., Jan.9 | DAY 6 Sat., Jan.10 | DAY 7 Sun., Jan.11 | DAY 8 Mon., Jan.12 | DAY 9 Tues., Jan.13 | DAY 10 Wed., Jan.14 | DAY 11 Thurs., Jan.15 | DAY 12 Fri., Jan. 16 | DAY 13 Sat., Jan.17 | DAY 14 Sun., Jan.18 | DAY 15 Mon., Jan.19 |

Daily precipitation levels for Montreal Island

Legend: 1998 levels, Normal levels

Precipitation fell as snow on these days, not as freezing rain.

| | DAY 1 Mon., Jan.5 | DAY 2 Tues., Jan.6 | DAY 3 Wed., Jan.7 | DAY 4 Thurs., Jan.8 | DAY 5 Fri., Jan.9 | DAY 6 Sat., Jan.10 | DAY 7 Sun., Jan.11 | DAY 8 Mon., Jan.12 | DAY 9 Tues., Jan.13 | DAY 10 Wed., Jan.14 | DAY 11 Thurs., Jan.15 | DAY 12 Fri., Jan.16 | DAY 13 Sat., Jan.17 | DAY 14 Sun., Jan.18 | DAY 15 Mon., Jan.19 |

Sources: Gazette reports, Hydro-Québec, Met-Tech, The Weather Channel, Environment Canada

Dean Tweed, Gazette

A blue jay finds shelter in a frozen cedar near Merrickville, Ontario. Jays and most other species of birds weathered the storm well, though grouse and partridges suffered losses. (Lynn Ball, Ottawa Citizen)

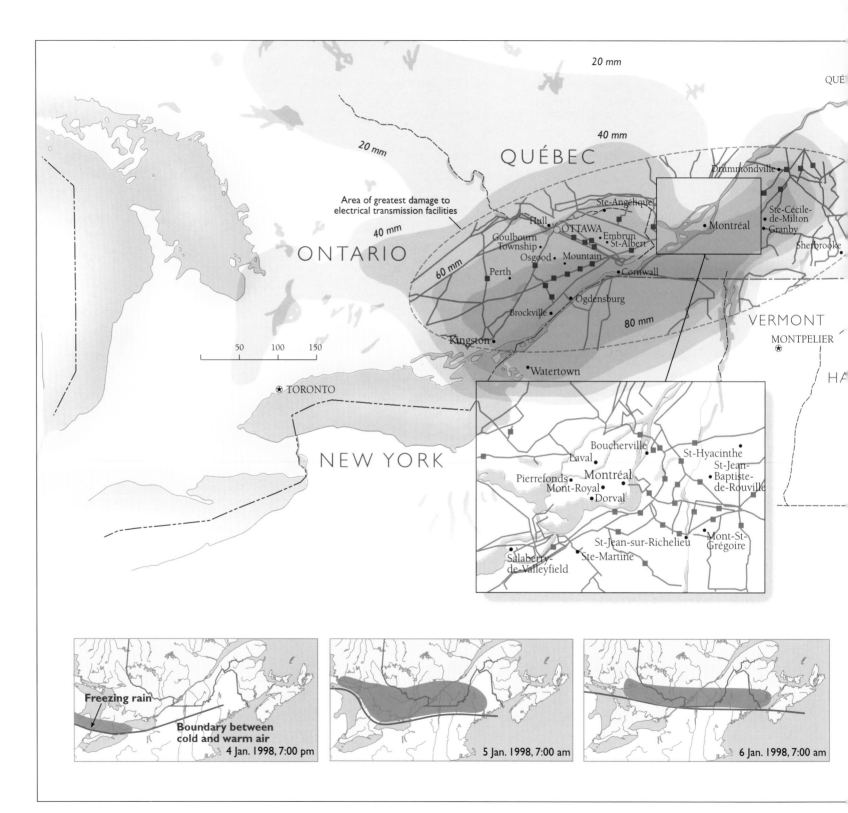

20 mm

QUÉ

20 mm

40 mm

QUÉBEC

Area of greatest damage to
electrical transmission facilities

40 mm

ONTARIO

Ste-Angélique

Hull OTTAWA
Goulbourn Embrun
Township St-Albert
Osgood Mountain

Drummondville

Ste-Cécile-
de-Milton
Montréal Granby

Sherbrooke

60 mm

Perth

Cornwall

80 mm

VERMONT

Ogdensburg

Brockville

Kingston

MONTPELIER

Watertown

50   100   150

TORONTO

Boucherville
Laval St-Hyacinthe
St-Jean-
Pierrefonds Baptiste-
Mont-Royal Montréal de-Rouville
Dorval

NEW YORK

St-Jean-sur-Richelieu Mont-St-
Grégoire
Salaberry-
de-Valleyfield Ste-Martine

HA

Freezing rain

Boundary between
cold and warm air
4 Jan. 1998, 7:00 pm

5 Jan. 1998, 7:00 am

6 Jan. 1998, 7:00 am

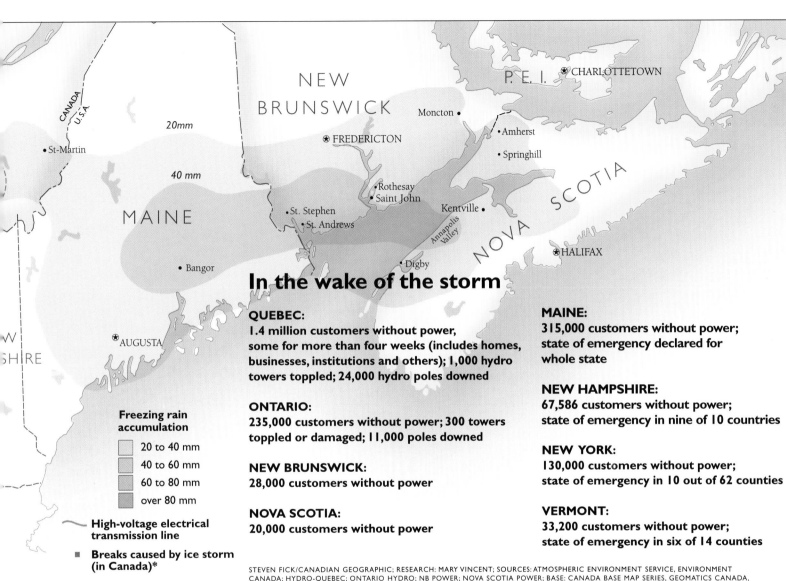

NEW BRUNSWICK

P. E. I. ✪ CHARLOTTETOWN

Moncton •

✪ FREDERICTON

• Amherst

• Springhill

20mm

40 mm

• St-Martin

MAINE

• Rothesay
• Saint John

• St. Stephen
• St. Andrews

Kentville •

Annapolis Valley

NOVA SCOTIA

✪ HALIFAX

• Bangor

• Digby

✪ AUGUSTA

CANADA
U.S.A.

In the wake of the storm

QUEBEC:
1.4 million customers without power, some for more than four weeks (includes homes, businesses, institutions and others); 1,000 hydro towers toppled; 24,000 hydro poles downed

ONTARIO:
235,000 customers without power; 300 towers toppled or damaged; 11,000 poles downed

NEW BRUNSWICK:
28,000 customers without power

NOVA SCOTIA:
20,000 customers without power

MAINE:
315,000 customers without power; state of emergency declared for whole state

NEW HAMPSHIRE:
67,586 customers without power; state of emergency in nine of 10 countries

NEW YORK:
130,000 customers without power; state of emergency in 10 out of 62 counties

VERMONT:
33,200 customers without power; state of emergency in six of 14 counties

Freezing rain accumulation

20 to 40 mm
40 to 60 mm
60 to 80 mm
over 80 mm

High-voltage electrical transmission line

■ Breaks caused by ice storm (in Canada)*

preliminary data

STEVEN FICK/CANADIAN GEOGRAPHIC; RESEARCH: MARY VINCENT; SOURCES: ATMOSPHERIC ENVIRONMENT SERVICE, ENVIRONMENT CANADA; HYDRO-QUEBEC; ONTARIO HYDRO; NB POWER; NOVA SCOTIA POWER; BASE: CANADA BASE MAP SERIES, GEOMATICS CANADA, NATURAL RESOURCES CANADA

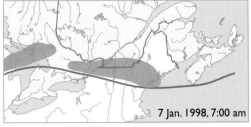

7 Jan. 1998, 7:00 am

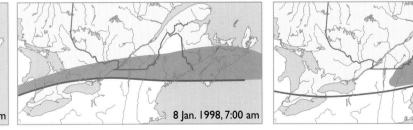

8 Jan. 1998, 7:00 am

9 Jan. 1998, 7:00 am

Chapter One

THE ORDEAL BEGINS

On the first morning of the ice, dead Christmas trees lay by the road-side, waiting for garbage trucks to come and pick them up. The holidays had finished; children and teenagers were heading back to classes, nervous and excited. The country seemed in a buoyant mood, its economy on the mend, national disunity far from most people's minds. A new year was underway, a millennium fast approaching. Optimism hung like sunlight in the air. But there was no sunlight that morning over much of eastern Canada: only a grey sky, a cascade of ice pellets and a rain that froze on impact.

At first this was a weather crisis. You can blame a rare split in the jet-stream, which had sent a huge mass of wet, warm air slithering north from the Gulf of Mexico. As this low-pressure air moved, it shed rain up the length of the United States. Then, on Monday, January 5, 1998, it hit the Great Lakes and the St. Lawrence River valley and came up against a dry belt of air coiling along the valley from Labrador and the Arctic.

The warm air rose and flowed northeast. Its high clouds continued to relinquish their moisture. But in the frigid air beneath, the rain cooled.

Left: Digging out was tough. Montreal's streets had not been cleared after a storm on December 30, and the freezing rain formed a thick layer of ice on top of the snowbanks, sidewalks and streets. (Dave Sidaway, The Gazette)

On day two of the rain, crews in Saint-Lambert, Quebec, were trying to clear the mess along des Saulniers Street. (Gordon Beck, The Gazette)

Isabelle Guibert of Outremont, Quebec, scrapes ice off her car window in hopes of getting the car out of the way of falling branches. (John Mahoney, The Gazette)

Supercooled, to be more precise: it stayed liquid even below the freezing point. As soon as this rain made contact with a cold object – a car, a tree-trunk, a roof, an electricity wire – it instantly froze until everything was sheathed in a thick layer of ice.

From the resort towns along Georgian Bay all the way eastward across the St. Lawrence River and almost as far as the coast of Maine, people that morning finished the last of their coffee and ventured out into the dirty weather that heralded the storm.

The ordeal began with a chipping away at the shield of ice obscuring windshields and car doors, or with a slow, precarious walk down roads and sidewalks that had turned overnight into skating rinks. As the rain continued, the ice thickened. Branches and trees began to fall, then

hydro poles; soon giant steel hydro towers lay crumpled on the ground. Power was cut off as the hydro system weakened. As the cold crept into their homes, thousands of people would seek refuge with friends and family or at emergency shelters. By the time the rain stopped, five days later, the storm had brought an entire region to a standstill, causing more than $1 billion in damage and disrupting the lives of millions. People in eastern Canada and the northeastern United States were left in the dark, cold, vulnerable, isolated and afraid.

That first day, January 5, classes in a few schools were cancelled, mainly in rural areas, but most children and adults tried to go about their normal duties. Rush-hour traffic was more congested than usual in Montreal and Ottawa; still, in a part of the world accustomed to ice and snow, the weather was little more than an annoyance.

The meteorologists knew better, and feared worse. In the small hours of the previous day, the Montreal weather office of Environment Canada had sent out a bulletin predicting the arrival of freezing rain. The data in the office's computers tell an ever-changing tale of air movements and temperature levels, humidity and pressure, fronts and precipitation. But the tale is hard for a layman to interpret, especially in winter, when snow and rain, ice pellets and freezing rain are all liable to drop from the heavens. There's nothing abnormal about freezing rain in the St. Lawrence valley. It falls a few times most winters, when wet and dry air masses collide.

Usually, the collision leads to one of the air masses blowing the other one away. Freezing rain seldom lasts for long. The fateful difference this time was that neither the cold air from the northeast nor the wet air from the south was about to pack up and move off. In the skies above Kingston and Brockville, Ottawa and Montreal, Granby and Saint-Hyacinthe, the warring clouds had settled in to stay. For five interminable days, the valley was their battleground.

There's more than one way to break the ice. Fritz Pierre, of Jeanne Mance Street in Montreal, goes at his windshield with a hammer. (Dave Sidaway, The Gazette)

When a scraper or hammer didn't cut it, John Abcarius used a spade to get the ice off the windshield of his car on Lincoln Avenue in Montreal. (Pierre Obendrauf, The Gazette)

"Out in the Atlantic near Bermuda," Environment Canada would later explain, "a large high-pressure system blocked the Gulf storms from following their normal track across the Atlantic and northward to Iceland, where most storms from North America die. Instead, like a boulder in a stream, the high pressure diverted the bulk of the moisture farther west along the western flank of the Appalachian Mountains directly into Ontario and Quebec where it collided with the cold Arctic air."

The storm's timing had an irony to it. Outside movie theatres all over the continent, people had been lining up for weeks to watch *Titanic*, the epic of a great ship – the largest ever built – that had rammed, top speed, into ice. If you believe the Céline Dion song, the heart carries on; not so the engineering. The finest equipment of the age – a grand symbol of a technological civilization – had proved helpless to resist a lump of frozen water. In more than one cinema of southwestern Quebec and eastern Ontario, *Titanic* was nearing its climax when the lights on the big screen, like the lights on the doomed vessel, flickered and went out. Pushing impatiently out of each blackened theatre, none of the frustrated customers knew how long this darkness was to last. The movie had allowed them to flirt with the disastrous power of ice. Now life was about to imitate art.

The blackouts began on Monday afternoon. They worsened through the night, knocking out power to thousands of homes as a hard rain continued to fall. Quebec was the prime victim; the weather through eastern Ontario was bad but not yet devastating. On Tuesday morning hundreds of thousands of Quebecers awoke in the dark and cold. Parents scrambled to find care for their children, as schools across much of southern Quebec had closed. In Papineauville, east of Hull, the ice storm had claimed its

These Hydro-Quebec pylons collapsed near Drummondville on January 7. (Alain Bédard, Le Nouvelliste)

first victim: 82-year-old Rolland Parent died of carbon monoxide poisoning while running a generator in the basement of his home.

Firefighters were busy at once. They had to deal with a small rash of house fires that erupted from power surges after the initial blackout. That morning alone, the 911 line received about 5,300 calls from Montrealers. Authorities put out an urgent appeal for people not to call 911 except in the case of genuine emergencies. Broken branches, they wearily explained, did not count as a genuine emergency.

But it wasn't just trees that were falling. Some transmission lines on the south shore of Montreal, an area that would soon become notorious as the "triangle of darkness," had already toppled under a brutal weight of ice. Airports were chaotic, freeways even more so. A high-voltage line collapsed near Drummondville, blocking the main highway between Quebec City and Montreal. Heavy salting along the Metropolitan Expressway succeeded only in flooding the road; cars inched across the island of Montreal in axle-deep water.

On Wednesday, the freezing rain lessened. Hydro-Quebec crews managed to give some blacked-out areas the respite of a few hours' heat and light. There was no respite on the South Shore, where hydro pylons lay twisted on the snow like abstract sculptures; as yet, however, no one realized the whole area would remain dark for weeks. As the temperature in many homes sank far below the comfort zone, the magnitude of the crisis was only gradually becoming clear. Shelters opened up; hotels

Montreal's St. Laurent Boulevard, the "Main," was jammed Friday, January 9, with people trying to get home. By late afternoon, 1.4 million customers were without power, ice bombs were flying off buildings in the downtown core forcing police to cordon off many city streets, authorities had closed all bridges to the South Shore, 46 regional highways were shut down, the city's water was unsafe for drinking and the entire water supply system was close to collapse. (Martin Chamberland, La Presse)

Trees loaded with ice near St. Joseph's Oratory in Montreal. (Robert Skinner, La Presse)

began to fill. In cities, towns and villages, emergency operation centres sprang into action. Or limped into action, for a lot of municipalities were painfully unready to face such a crisis.

The day wore on, the wind rose, and with it, the level of anxiety. More power lines tumbled. When the ice knocked out a major substation in Saint-Hyacinthe, more than one million people on the south shore were left in the dark. By late evening, hundreds of thousands of Montrealers had joined them.

And still the worst was yet to come. Inside their bright computer-filled office, the meteorologists couldn't hear the sirens, the car horns, the persistent moaning and cracking of the trees. That evening, Environment Canada forecasters in Montreal warned of a weather system that "will affect most regions tonight and Thursday. It will give important additional quantities of freezing rain." Like Cassandra in the Trojan War, they were able to foresee the dark future, but incapable of changing it.

The next day, Montreal dodged a bullet. It was Ottawa's turn to suffer. Spared the earlier brunt of the freezing rain, the capital now received almost an inch of it. The statues on Parliament Hill developed a thick coat of ice. By noon, most government departments had sent their employees home, leaving downtown Ottawa strangely desolate. A walk that normally lasted five minutes now took much longer. The lights went out in the homes of the prime minister and governor-general, just as they had two days earlier in the Outremont residence of Quebec's premier.

Outlying communities in the Ottawa Valley were even harder hit, and a potent combination of ice and wind destroyed nearly two-thirds of the transmission capacity for eastern Ontario. Early Thursday morning, the main line feeding Brockville failed, knocking out the city and many smaller communities nearby. The culprit was intense wind, hurtling across the St. Lawrence River and Lake Ontario. On Wolfe Island, a ferry

A tractor in Wolford Township, Ontario, shows the sheer weight of ice. The area south of Ottawa was badly hit by the storm. (Lynn Ball, Ottawa Citizen)

Desolation in a Montreal-area park. (Dave Sidaway, The Gazette)

ride away from the ravaged city of Kingston, the wind felled 300 hydro poles and left the islanders reeling in the dark.

Via Rail cancelled all trains east of Toronto; airlines cancelled many of their flights. Partisan politics became irrelevant: the only thing that counted now was help. After Quebec Premier Lucien Bouchard accepted a federal offer to send in the army, soldiers were soon deployed across a broad swath of southern Quebec as well as eastern Ontario. In Ontario they would be joined by hundreds of linemen from elsewhere in the province and beyond, and in Quebec by hundreds of hydro workers from other provinces and the United States. The number of troops would grow for days to come.

The extreme conditions even undermined the neutral tone of weather reports: Environment Canada issued a bulletin that warned of a further wave of precipitation "invading" the south of Quebec. Bernard Derome, Peter Mansbridge, Lloyd Robertson and other TV anchormen donned heavy coats and hats so as to broadcast live from the eye of the storm. A good part of their audience in Quebec and Ontario, however, lacked the electricity to watch the performance.

The worst day for Quebec came on Friday, January 9. "C'est l'enfer," read the front-page headline in La Presse. And indeed, the region looked and felt as though hell had frozen over. Nearly 1.4 million homes and businesses in Quebec were without power – the highest number during the whole crisis – as well as more than 230,000 in Ontario. Southwestern Quebec had been pounded again by freezing rain that had brought its hydro system to the brink of collapse. Only

Montreal Urban Community police constables Stefan Bisson (left) and John Boersma lift a pyjama-clad man over a snowbank while bringing him back to his LaSalle apartment building, evacuated because of the presence of carbon monoxide. (John Mahoney, The Gazette)

The full impact of the ice storm on birds and wildlife has not yet been measured. Some birds, like grouse and partridge, may have been hit hard because the ice-encased tree buds made food hard to come by. Squirrels, too, may have suffered if their food reserves were coated with ice. But the regenerative powers of nature are great. As for this little squirrel in Châteauguay, it just seemed to want to get out of the rain. (Phillip Norton)

one of five lines that fed power to Montreal was still standing and Hydro-Quebec, rather than risk the disintegration of what remained, cut off the electricity supply, plunging large parts of the downtown core and west end into darkness.

Blackouts crippled water-filtration plants and authorities were warning citizens to boil their water, if they could. People thronged grocery stores to buy bottled water and stock up on food. Police were going door-to-door in search of people who might need help finding shelter. Massive sheets of ice slid off the tops of buildings and bridges, forcing civil security authorities to cordon off much of the downtown core and close all the bridges to the South Shore. Outside the city it was no better: 46 regional highways were shut down.

Yet it wasn't just practical difficulties that inspired anxiety. Part of the hell, "l'enfer" that La Presse and the other newspapers wrote about, was fear: fear of the weather, fear of chaos, fear that the systems and networks that hold our society together were simply falling apart.

The storm respected no human boundaries. South of the U.S. border, parts of New Hampshire, Vermont and northern New York were also badly affected, not just by ice and freezing rain but by rivers overflowing their banks. On Friday, after punching one last fist in the face of millions, the storm finally left the St. Lawrence valley and pushed eastward. It knocked out power to tens of thousands of customers in Nova Scotia and New Brunswick, wreaking temporary havoc on Saint John. Nova Scotia, on the whole, got off lightly. In contrast, the entire state of Maine had fallen under a state of emergency (it would soon be declared a disaster area). By chance, ABC-TV was holding auditions that day in Southwest Harbor, Maine, for an upcoming mini-series. The name of the mini-series: "Storm of the Century."

That Friday in Montreal, the rain felt brittle. Dead Christmas trees had still not been picked up; but now they were hidden by further debris and

At first, it was the beauty that was most striking. But as the ice took over, beauty turned to devastation. Here, ice blankets the trees on Mount Royal around the Women's Pavilion of the Royal Victoria Hospital in Montreal. (Dave Sidaway, The Gazette)

ice. Few vehicles were on the downtown streets. A lone bicycle courier tried to manoeuvre his way across the slippery ice on René Lévesque Boulevard. A flash of lightning suddenly lit up the grey sky above Old Montreal, followed by a roll of thunder. A few seconds later, another flash appeared over Chinatown. The glassy rain had turned into ice pellets; or was that hail? Whatever the precipitation was, it hurt. Thunder in January? Apocalypse now? It seemed briefly, irrationally, possible that the end was nigh.

A lot of people had the same suspicion. "The weather, it's the power of God," an immigrant from Panama told a Montreal Gazette reporter in a candlelit pub. "I am understanding now what is really happening in life – the end is coming."

Montreal bicycle courier Sylvain Moisan could only push his bike to his next delivery on St. Antoine Street during rush hour on Friday, January 9. Even so, trudging through the snow on foot was faster than going by car.
(Pierre Obendrauf, The Gazette)

It could take years for the landscape to recover. (André Pichette, The Gazette)

Above: By sunrise, Tuesday, January 6, large pockets of southwestern Quebec, the Outaouais and eastern Ontario were without power as rain turned into an escalating ice storm, downing thousands of tree branches and hydro lines. Every school board in and around Montreal was closed. In Papineauville, east of Hull, the ice storm had claimed its first victim: 82-year-old Rolland Parent succumbed to carbon monoxide poisoning while running a gas generator in the basement of his home. Fear was mounting. In this photo, Côte St. Luc firefighters had to negotiate streets littered with broken branches in order to respond to calls. (Richard Arless, The Gazette)

Left: Lafontaine Park in Montreal. (Pierre McCann, La Presse)

Schools across Ontario and Quebec were shut down because of the ice storm. In Quebec, 440,000 students missed classes in more than 1,900 schools and colleges, some of which were closed for up to 23 days. In Ontario, 553 schools shut down, some for up to 12 days. For Alison Ferguson of Wolford Township, missing school wasn't entirely a holiday. Her family farm was blacked out, so she had to help with the chores and feed a calf by bottle, while her father used a generator to milk his herd. (Lynn Ball, Ottawa Citizen)

Above: Frozen trucks lined up near Saint-Jean-Baptiste-de-Rouville, Quebec.
(Dave Sidaway, The Gazette)

Left: Tree limbs and branches snapped like twigs under the weight of the ice. On Wednesday, January 7, when this photo was shot, the worst was yet to come.
(John Mahoney, The Gazette)

Ice Chrysler. (Phillip Norton)

Left: Ronald's icy nose and frozen smile brought a few chuckles to customers at the McDonald's restaurant in Bells Corners, Ontario. (Wayne Hiebert, Ottawa Citizen)

Below: After the rain, this car lot in Châteauguay, Quebec, looked like an ice sculpture. (Phillip Norton)

Life goes on. Jesse McKellar was born near the lighthouse on St. Laurent Boulevard in Ottawa at 7:32 a.m. on January 6. The ice storm made driving so difficult that his parents, Tasha Geymonat and Jody McKellar of Edwards, Ontario, didn't reach a hospital in time. Baby and parents did just fine. (Wayne Hiebert, Ottawa Citizen)

Nelson Street in Kingston on Friday, January 9. (Ian MacAlpine, Kingston Whig-Standard)

Fallen wires and icy conditions made driving on Léon-Hamel Street in Granby impossible. This picture was taken on January 12, a week after the storm began.
(Alain Dion, La Voix de l'Est)

Like everything else in Ottawa, the Agricultural Museum was under a sheet of ice.
(Malak, Ottawa Citizen)

Above: Branches and hydro wires block Pine Street at the corner of Orchard Street in Brockville on Thursday, January 8.
(Ronald Zajac, Brockville Recorder and Times)

Left: When the storm hit, many people still had their Christmas lights up, like these on Brockville's Court House Green. The spire in the background above the bent trees is that of the First Presbyterian Church.
(Phil Kall, Brockville Recorder and Times)

Left: A car damaged by a broken tree limb near Victoria Park in Kingston.
(Ian MacAlpine, Kingston Whig-Standard)

Right: Nature played no favourites. A pickup truck, Nature's Choice, sits crumpled under a fallen tree in a parking lot on Lisgar Street in Ottawa. (Julie Oliver, Ottawa Citizen)

Above: Motorists in the Montreal suburb of Lachine had to dodge fallen branches. (Dave Sidaway, The Gazette)

Right: A snapped hydro pole was part of the destruction along Stanley Street in Saint-Lambert, Quebec. (John Kenney, The Gazette)

Above: Kingston under ice. (Ian MacAlpine, Kingston Whig-Standard)

Left: A window of beauty in the small Quebec community of Saint-Jean-Baptiste-de-Rouville. (Dave Sidaway, The Gazette)

Travel by car, train and air was risky during the storm. Three days after the freezing rain began, passengers on a commuter train from Rigaud had to walk half a mile to the Dorval Station to continue on to downtown Montreal by bus. (Peter Cooney, The Gazette)

No hot air blowing here. Politicians were back in their ridings when the ice storm hit Parliament Hill. (Malak, Ottawa Citizen)

The moon was the only thing lighting up Sainte-Julie on the south shore of Montreal on January 12. (John Kenney, The Gazette)

Chapter Two

IN THE WAR ZONE

"Finally now we're doing something helpful, as opposed to just training all the time. I mean, today all we were going to do is throw grenades. And we always throw grenades, and that gets boring."

– A soldier newly arrived in Chelsea, Quebec

The trees were on Bob Petch's mind. For decades he has run a fruit farm just outside Hemmingford, a small town in the Châteauguay Valley in southern Quebec. Petch is famous for his apples: not just the usual McIntoshes, Cortlands and Spartans, but also rare heirloom varieties like Gravensteins, Wolf Rivers and Cox's Orange Pippins. When he was asked about the ice storm months later, he wanted to talk about his trees.

"The vegetation, it's terrible. We made an estimate of our orchard damage, and among the standard trees – the big, old ones – there was 37 per cent damage. The maple trees are broken, too. The poplars are all stripped – just toothpicks sticking up in the air. The birches bent over in

Left: Apple trees are used to the weight of fruit but some trees could not withstand the load of ice that covered them. This orchard is in Rougemont, famous for its apples and juice. It was one of the hardest-hit areas in Quebec.
(Denis Courville, La Presse)

In warmer times, Bob Petch in his apple grove near Hemmingford, Quebec.
(Richard Arless, The Gazette)

the ice, and a lot of them are still bent over. We have an old elm, a beautiful one, but the top's all gone now – the branches would have fallen a hundred feet. It's the spruces that've come off the best of any kind of tree: the ice only took a few feet off the top."

Petch took some pictures on the last day of the storm. One of them is a close-up of a young branch, the size of a pencil in diameter. Normally, he explains, you'd find an icicle hanging down off a twig like that. But the ice storm laid "a good three and a half inches of ice on top of that branch." Small wonder that in the Hemmingford area, some of the sugar-maple bushes suffered crippling damage. The ice sheared the tops off the trees, leaving hardly enough to draw up the sap. Storm damage in some areas left the woods looking as dark and broken as if a fire had swept through.

Farmers, at a time like this, seldom whine. They just get on with the job at hand. But don't misunderstand the lack of complaint. The storm was devastating to many of them in Quebec and Ontario alike. Dairy farmers struggled to milk their herds, and had to throw out millions of litres of milk. Maple trees were ruined. Thousands of pigs, chickens and other livestock died. Greenhouses went cold. Some farmers worked day and night to avert such losses. Not only were they among the worst-affected by the crisis: they were also among the last to see the power restored. It would take the better part of a year for fruit growers to discover the full extent of the damage they had sustained.

Something of the farmers' traditional self-reliance, their sturdy independence of spirit, could be found in small communities, too. West of Montreal, the stricken town of Hudson united in a heart-stirring way.

Left: Apple orchards like this one on Route 235 in Ange-Gardien were damaged by the weight of the ice. Twigs the size of pencils were coated with ice as thick as your wrist after five days of relentless freezing rain.
(Michel St-Jean, La Voix de l'Est)

Above: Marian Lenczewski of Friends of the Earth wept when she saw half a "splendid green ash" in Metcalfe, Ontario, lying on the ground. (Pat McGrath, Ottawa Citizen)

Right: Mark Wheeler, part owner of Wheeler Pancake House and Sugar Camp near McDonalds Corners, Ontario, surveys the storm damage to his sugar bush. Some maple groves in Quebec and Ontario were severely damaged.
(Dave Mullington, Ottawa Citizen)

When a 50-foot tree hit his house in the middle of the night, novelist Trevor Ferguson said, "Neighbours with flashlights came running from all over. They wanted to make sure we were OK." He was speaking a week after the storm; it would be another week before Hudson – most of it – regained power. "People do come together, those who know each other, and those who don't. Pumps and generators are being passed from house to house. Everyone is looking out for everyone else."

The rebuilding in country areas occurred one road at a time, one system at a time. Before the electricity came back, telephone service was restored. Before the phones came back, the water supply was fixed. A working phone enabled you to share news of your predicament with friends and relatives, near and far. A safe supply of water meant that you no longer needed to fetch and carry it from pumps. Even better, you could take a shower at home. The people of Hemmingford endured four days without water before a generator from Albany, New York, got the town's well back in operation. The irony was lost on nobody: a crisis brought on by the power of water had led to no power and no water. In some of the more remote areas, people blessed with generators welcomed a steady stream of neighbours to their door, each one clutching a towel and fresh clothes, each one in need of a shower.

Maybe this pulling together, this sharing, this mutual support that appeared to be so wonderfully typical in rural districts – maybe it was only human nature. In his book *Natural Hazards*, Edward Bryant suggests it's a myth "that people experiencing the calamity appear confused, are stunned and helpless. If anything, disasters bring out the strength in people . . . The victims are more than capable of organizing themselves and performing the rescue work. The only things they may lack are the tools to carry out the task efficiently."

After the ice storm, the most useful tools of all were wood stoves and generators. But it wasn't just efficiency that came to the fore; it was practical ingenuity. What happened in the little town of Alfred, 70 kilometres east of Ottawa, is typical. The day the storm brutalized the Ottawa Valley, all power died in the community. Fallen branches lay in tangles over the crumpled wires; businesses and restaurants closed down. But what would happen to the 80 or so old people living in Auberge Plein Soleil and Pension du Bonheur?

Alfred didn't wait for outside intervention. It didn't wait to be told what to do. Instead the town's mayor, Jean-Claude Trottier, had an idea. With some friends, he dug the enormous generator for a summer carnival – Carousel Amusements by name – out of the frozen snow in a local field. Trottier transported it, with two backhoes, to the darkened Knights of Columbus hall. There the town created an instant shelter, complete with mattresses from a nearby school and hot meals prepared by a local caterer. Apart from the residents of the seniors' homes, more than 100 other people took refuge at the hall within hours of Trottier's inspiration.

In a small town like Alfred, it's hard to keep anything secret. Word spreads fast. But in larger centres, authorities faced the extra challenge of reaching a public that was not only starved for warmth and light, but also short of information. Saint-Jean-sur-Richelieu has about 40,000 people, but no daily newspaper or radio station. The city council had thousands of brochures printed up elsewhere, brochures it quickly distributed at corner stores: "Restez chez vous autant que faire se peut. Dépannez-vous entre voisins, organisez des réseaux de solidarité." (Stay home as much as possible. Help out your neighbours. Organize networks of solidarity.) The imperative mood reflected the urgency of the moment.

The crisis turned many people into reluctant nomads. When the power went out in her home in Greenfield Park, a south shore suburb of

A month after the storm, Montreal mayor Pierre Bourque tours piles of broken trees and branches on Mount Royal. (John Kenney, The Gazette)

It was hard to keep clean during the blackout. Pierre Wilson is all smiles as he steps out squeaky clean from a car wash in Saint-Luc, Quebec. Owner Denis Dauray transformed his car wash into showers – 10 for men and 10 for women – using a generator to heat the water. (Pierre McCann, La Presse)

Montreal, Chantale Cyr, her partner and their 14-month-old son went to stay in the Gatineau region. A couple of days later the power died there, too, so the family moved back towards home, staying with relatives in La Prairie. That's where Jason, the little boy, badly burned his hand on a woodstove. After doctors bandaged him up in a hospital, the family moved once more, to stay with Cyr's mother in Saint-Hubert. It was their fourth home in less than a week.

Except in the major cities, the necessities were not always easy to find. Dozens of people formed a line outside a bargain store in Brockville as soon as the local radio station announced that the store had candles for sale. When gasoline grew scarce in the town, lineups at the pumps lasted as long as three hours. Without electricity, life became not just colder but also simpler, more sharply focused, as though the crisis had forced modern citizens to revert to the ancient status of hunter-gatherers. The search for water and food, the quest for fire: such atavistic pursuits filled the days of men and women whose waking hours are usually passed in front of a classroom or before a computer screen. Now they became foragers.

"It was like a war zone here," Bob Petch recalled. Many other people in affected towns and cities used the same figure of speech. Across the whole region, the enemy took more than 30 casualties, mainly among older people: deaths by hypothermia and carbon monoxide poisoning, deaths by housefires and ice falls. Against this particular enemy, we had no stronger weapon than the chainsaw. The widespread sense of living in the midst of conflict was all the more appropriate, perhaps, in that the storm provoked the largest domestic operation in the history of Canada's armed forces. Up to 16,000 troops and reservists from across the country took part.

Not since the FLQ crisis of 1970 had the army been deployed on the streets of Montreal. Operation Recuperation, as it was called, found veterans of Bosnia and Haiti plucking branches off city streets. At first the military's role seemed more than a trifle unclear, its movements more than a trifle uncoordinated. But before long, especially in rural areas, the soldiers came into their own. They used helicopters to airlift the sick and injured to hospital in Kingston; they built temporary housing for hydro crews in Hawkesbury; they worked beside and ahead of hydro workers on the south shore of Montreal, clearing away debris so that the linemen could reconstruct the power network as fast as possible. Lucien Bouchard

When the lights went out, people found all kinds of ways to keep warm and keep things running. In Boucherville, Quebec, two CN diesel locomotives parked on a street served as giant generators for city hall and a local school. (André Pichette, The Gazette)

was quick to praise the soldiers' "absolutely exceptional" work in the triangle of darkness.

"The army's help is extraordinarily important," said Renée Legendre, the mayor of the town of Carignan, a week after the storm. "Everybody has to be told that." She was thankful to the army for opening up a second shelter and a camp kitchen – Carignan's original shelter was full to bursting point, and some families had adopted the dangerous habit of sleeping in their cars. Amid a growing sense of anxiety in Carignan, the army had also helped to re-establish a feeling of calm; a confidence that one day, if not tomorrow, or even next week, normal life would return.

Above: When the power went out, so did the gas pumps. People in the Brockville area lined up for hours to buy gas at Korim's General Store at Row's Corners on Friday, January 9. In this picture, the line up is one kilometre long.
(Deanna Clark, Brockville Recorder and Times)

Left: Dan Galarneau, Dr. Ben Leikin and his son, Ben, pull a downed branch off the road in front of the Leikin home on Mayfair Street in Ottawa.
(Lynn Ball, Ottawa Citizen)

Above: Farmers were especially hard hit by the storm, forced to seek shelter for their cattle as well as their families. Spencerville, Ontario, dairy farmer Bill Lawrence, shown here with one of his cows, had to move his animals to the farm of his neighbour, Doug Cleary, during the blackout.
(Mark Calder, Brockville Recorder and Times)

Left: Margaret Henry keeps warm during the blackout with her goats and cats at her candlelit home in Ramsay Township, Ontario.
(Bruno Schlumberger, Ottawa Citizen)

Soldiers in freezing cold help with hydro repairs.
(Belinda Foster, Cornwall Standard Freeholder)

Captain Ross Bradley of the Royal Canadian Regiment from Gagetown, New Brunswick, briefs members of H Company after their arrival in Saint-Jean-sur-Richelieu, Quebec. Gagetown sent 650 soldiers to the affected area. (Gordon Beck, The Gazette)

Above: A young hockey fan greets soldiers arriving in Saint-Hyacinthe, Quebec.
(John Kenney, The Gazette)

Left: The military collected transformer parts to recycle.
(Armand Trottier, La Presse)

These soldiers had good reason to smile. The residents of Saint-Césaire in Quebec's triangle of darkness, where this photo was taken, greeted them with open arms when they arrived to help restore the hydro lines. (Alain Dion, La Voix de l'Est)

2nd Lt. Phil Halton, Royal Canadian Dragoons, Petawawa, directs traffic near Osgoode, Ontario, while hydro workers repaired lines on January 15 in a windchill of minus 40C (minus 40 Fahrenheit). (Lynn Ball, Ottawa Citizen)

The military presence served to reassure many people frightened by the storm and the blackout. Here, a military helicopter lands behind the community centre in Metcalfe, Ontario. (Chris Mikula, Ottawa Citizen)

Above: Defence Minister Art Eggleton (right) in his storm gear confers with Colonel Craig McQuitty, commanding officer of the Brockville Rifles. Eggleton flew into Brockville by helicopter on January 12 for a briefing on what the region needed. (Nick Gardiner, Brockville Recorder and Times)

Right: Cpl. Mike McColeman carries Alex Dow, 79, from his rural home near Metcalfe, Ontario, into an emergency vehicle waiting to take him to the local hospital. (Wayne Cuddington, Ottawa Citizen)

A soldier tries to free downed wires near Saint-Césaire, Quebec. More than 3,000 kilometres of Quebec's power network broke down. (Paul Chiasson, Canadian Press)

In Goulburn, Ontario, Ann Carruthers had been trapped in her home, where she lives alone, without heat or power for three days. Troops finally freed her, clearing trees that had blocked her laneway. (Bruno Schlumberger, Ottawa Citizen)

Gabriel Rouleau, 4, gets a hug from Capt. Johanne Dostie at the general headquarters of the Canadian Forces Base in Saint-Jean-sur-Richelieu, Quebec. The boy is one of many kids who stayed at the headquarters from the start of the ice storm because there was no power at his home. (Bruno Schlumberger, Ottawa Citizen)

Chapter Three

REVIVING MONTREAL

"Closed until the end of the apocalypse."
— A sign in the window of Movie Land, a Montreal video store

But Movie Land reopened much sooner than that. Indeed, the store reopened while most of its regular customers were still in the dark, and while the provincial government was urging shops and offices in downtown Montreal to remain shut. The government wanted to cut the risk of overloading the precarious electricity system; one way to do that was by asking people to keep away from the area. But the people had other ideas. Their experience of the ice storm would say a lot about the character of Montreal. Short of imposing martial law, it's hard to keep a great city down by decree.

Near the end of the freezing rain, the temperature began to rise. Friday, January 9, while miserable, was a little warmer than Thursday, Saturday warmer still. But when the air thawed, the ice bombs started to fall. Chunks of ice, some of them weighing 50 pounds or more, catapulted off the tops of buildings. Walking was hazardous. To avoid a serious tumble, you had to watch the slippery ground; to avoid the falling

Marc Therrien holds a piece of ice taken from the belfry tower at Montreal's City Hall. (Robert Mailloux, La Presse)

Left: Firefighters clear ice from a roof in Old Montreal on de la Commune Street, near Notre Dame Basilica. (Phillip Norton)

ice, you had to look sideways and up; to avoid fellow pedestrians, and to figure out where you were going, you had to glance ahead occasionally. As they worked to clear the debris or simply plodded to the corner store to buy the essentials – bread, beer, batteries – some people wore hard hats or bicycle helmets.

Drivers had their challenges, too. The police blocked roads for the purpose of de-icing, turning much of the city into an elaborate labyrinth and closing off large parts of the downtown core and Old Montreal. News reports had told of a woman in Saint-Martin-de-Beauce in southeastern Quebec who had been killed by a falling slab of ice. Even in a car, the prospect of being hit by an ice bomb was no joke. But then in 18th-century Russia, whole cannons had been constructed of ice, strong enough to withstand the explosion of a quarter-pound of powder with an iron ball.

That weekend, after the storm, the sun briefly reappeared. The weather forecasters were adamant: no more freezing rain. Reason enough for a modest celebration: candlelit dinners for two, an early night in bed. In some churches, candlelit services drew a greater number of worshippers than show up on a regular Sunday. Prayer was not a bad idea; the energy supply to Montreal – and, for that matter, Ottawa – was still hanging by a thread. The Rolling Stones concert in Montreal's Olympic Stadium had to be called off; so did performances by Oasis, Helmut Lotti and the Montreal Canadiens.

Traffic in Montreal was still moving cautiously. Many roads were cluttered by smashed-up trees and iced-in cars. A high proportion of traffic

Pedestrians had to dodge falling ice in Old Montreal and in the downtown core, parts of which were shut down while crews knocked the ice off roofs and street lamps. This photo of St. Sulpice Street and Notre Dame Basilica was shot on January 15, 10 days after the freezing rain began. (André Pichette, The Gazette)

lights no longer functioned. Police patrols were increased: throughout the crisis, the crime rate stayed low.

As more and more homes grew distressingly cold, hotels and motels became a popular option – for those who were able and willing to pay the price. Many hotels were fully occupied by local guests, and to meet their needs the hotels improvised fast. The Oval Room in the elegant Ritz-Carlton Hotel was transformed into an activities centre for children, its socialites and debutantes temporarily replaced by clowns. "We consider the hotel like a cruise ship," said the manager, Carel Folkersma. A cruise ship with a blazing fireplace, that is.

A few blocks away stands Ben's Delicatessen, a Montreal landmark since its founding in 1908. The Kravitz family ran it then and runs it still. Al Kravitz, who is almost as old as the restaurant itself, is convinced that during all that time, Ben's had never closed for more than a day. But on the black Friday of January 9, the power went out. It would stay out for most of the weekend. Although the light and heat reappeared on Sunday afternoon, Al's sister-in-law, Jean Kravitz, said, "We weren't going to open right away. But the phone, it didn't stop! We got so many calls from people stranded in hotels that we just had to open." And so, the next morning, chopped-liver sandwiches and Cherry Cokes were again being served at the corner of Metcalfe and de Maisonneuve, just as they have for generations. Tattered Christmas snowflakes hung from the ceiling.

The power supply was still so fragile that Premier Bouchard urged businesses in the heart of Montreal to remain closed and people to stay away, and the big enterprises obeyed: banks, universities, head offices, department stores. Yet a sex shop reopened on Ste. Catherine Street West; across the road, a medical practice was open, too. A dollar store

One week later, crews were still removing ice from Notre Dame Basilica and other buildings in Old Montreal. (Gordon Beck, The Gazette)

On Friday, January 9, as temperatures began to rise, large sheets and chunks of ice began falling from the tops of bridges. Bridges from Montreal to the South Shore were closed for two days while crews de-iced them. (Bernard Brault, La Presse)

near the Guy station of the subway network had neither heat nor light, but a woman stood shivering in her winter coat by the door, continuing to sell whatever shoehorns and mousetraps, lipstick and party favours her customers could find in the chilly semi-darkness. You couldn't see much at the back of the store except your own breath. Outside, the usual lineup for the 165 bus stretched halfway down the road.

"Why are people here?" asked a genial panhandler, standing outside the closed Eaton's store. "I have no idea. But I have to say, in this whole blackout, business hasn't been bad." He was pleased and a little surprised to find he had no competition. "This little stretch," the man said with a grin, "is usually full of bums."

And so, fitfully, spasmodically, Montreal lurched back to life. The process was slow and difficult: in the wake of the ice storm, the partial melt and the arctic chill that followed, granite-like mountains of ice knocked 30 per cent of the city's snow-removal equipment out of action. Normally this would have caused a scandal, or at least a controversy. But now, people were too busy to protest. Politics could wait. There was no outstanding moment, no dramatic symbol of the city's return to health; just a gradual reawakening, a slow shaking-off of the trauma, one street, one block, one sidewalk at a time.

When the power did come back, relief sometimes mingled with sheer unbridled joy. "I'm going to live life at 100 miles an hour," cried 65-year-old Denise Payette. She had spent a week in the dark, the temperature of her Notre-Dame-de-Grâce home dropping almost to the freezing point, the smell of spoiled food in her refrigerator growing more and more obtrusive. "I'll do everything I want now! I'll spend my money! I'm going to do all sorts of crazy things!"

Above: Like most of Montreal, Chinatown was blacked out and its restaurants forced to close. Here, people wait for a bus in Chinatown.
(John Kenney, The Gazette)

Right: A woman clambers over some of the huge blocks of ice that clogged the streets of Montreal for weeks after the storm. Clean-up was slow and difficult. The mountains of ice knocked out 30 per cent of the city's snow-removal equipment. (Paul Chiasson, Canadian Press)

A worker kicks ice from a ledge in Old Montreal.
(John Kenney, The Gazette)

The ice storm left Montreal's flat roofs packed solid with ice, in some cases up to a foot thick. This man tackled the ice on the roof of La Presse in Old Montreal with a pickaxe, but many others used sledgehammers or chain-saws. (Jean Goupil, La Presse)

Ice from buildings, trees and bridges fell like swords from the sky, shutting roads and parts of Montreal for days. Here, a firefighter breaks the ice off a lamppost on Ste. Catherine Street. (André Pichette, The Gazette)

It took weeks for people to clear the thick ice from their roofs, driveways and walkways. Sébastien Boulianne of Brossard, Quebec, smashes the ice in his driveway with an axe while his brother Frédéric (right) and a friend, Marc-André Lacroix (centre), clear it away.
(André Pichette, The Gazette)

Above: Charles Brocklehurst boosts the candlelight with a flashlight to help Elizabeth Maloney read from the Bible during mass in the chapel at St. Patrick's Basilica in Montreal. (John Mahoney, The Gazette)

Left: Anything to keep warm. This Westmount family, Mahaya Boicel (left), Roukouchi Boicel (right) and mother Gemma Mattheij slept in a tent in their living-room and used each other's body heat to keep warm during the blackout. (Phil Carpenter, The Gazette)

Right: Two people team up to free a trapped car in the Montreal neighbourhood of Saint-Henri. (Robert Skinner, La Presse)

Left: A crane, used to remove the ice from the roof of the Ritz-Carlton Hotel, topples over at the corner of Sherbrooke and Drummond streets in Montreal.
(André Pichette, The Gazette)

Right: The storm delayed normal street-cleaning operations in Montreal. As late as January 25, Garnier Street posed a challenge to drivers, cyclists and pedestrians alike.
(Robert Skinner, La Presse)

This driver has to contend with small mountains of ice and hard-packed snow on Chateaubriand Street in Montreal. (Robert Skinner, La Presse)

When two hands aren't enough, Louise Caillier uses her head.
Here, she was rushing through the storm debris to catch a bus
on Park Avenue near Mount Royal Avenue, in Montreal.
(John Kenney, The Gazette)

Above: Some things won't wait, even in an ice storm. Cairo the whippet is dressed for winter weather on a walk with owner Carlos Carrascosa. (John Kenney, The Gazette)

Left: Courier Charles Masson heaves his bicycle over a Montreal snowbank. (Dave Sidaway, The Gazette)

Montreal buses were slowed to a crawl and half the subway system in Montreal was shut down by blackouts. Here, commuters trying to get home on Friday, January 9, wait for a bus on René Lévesque Boulevard at the corner of Bleury Street beneath shattered trees. (Pierre Obendrauf, The Gazette)

Left: Beautiful Biosphere at the Expo '67 site on Ile Ste. Hélène in the St. Lawrence River. (Gordon Beck, The Gazette)

Above: But getting the ice off it was no easy trick. (Martin Chamberland, La Presse)

Chapter Four

THE KINDNESS OF STRANGERS

"Dear Mayor and council, city of Ottawa: My brother and I have sent you our allowance to help with the ice storm. We lost our power too, for $3\frac{1}{2}$ days. Sincerely, Joshua and Christopher"

The two boys, seven and nine years old, live in Quispamsis, a village about 20 kilometres north of Saint John, New Brunswick. Joshua and Christopher taped a two-dollar coin to their letter and mailed it to "The Mayor, city of Ottawa, Ottawa, Ont." Surprisingly, perhaps, it got through. The coin joined all the other donations to the region's disaster relief fund, donations sent from across Canada and beyond.

In the wake of the storm, big businesses as well as small boys displayed an unusual willingness to help out. Molson and Labatt came up with coupons you could use to replace any beer that had frozen and spoiled in the absence of power. The Royal Bank in the little Ontario town of Metcalfe set up a special account to assist a local dairy farmer whose new, half-million-dollar dairy barn had collapsed under the weight of ice. There were dozens, hundreds, thousands of such stories. Images and stories of the crisis had touched people's hearts; to help was a downright

Left: Kerry Goral, 2, found a new friend in Anna Francsek while playing at the shelter at Loyola High School in Montreal. (Pierre Obendrauf, The Gazette)

When people want to help, the only language spoken is compassion. Lumberjack Aimé Beaudoin from the Gaspé, Gaëtan Boisselle of Sorel, Quebec, and soldier Rob Gallagher from Edmonton, Alberta, team up to cut logs for residents of Saint-Luc, Quebec, who were blacked out for weeks. (Marie-France Coallier, The Gazette)

Above: A truck that was transporting firewood to blacked-out regions of Quebec toppled over on an icy stretch of Route 40 near Louiseville. The driver was not hurt. (Alain Bédard, Le Nouvelliste)

Left: Hundreds of volunteers across Quebec, Ontario and the northeastern United States, like Franco Serraiulo in the triangle of darkness, chopped firewood to heat homes during the blackouts. (Michel St-Jean, La Voix de l'Est)

pleasure. Hundreds of volunteers from all over the lightly affected Mauricie region of central Quebec descended on the isolated town of La Tuque to saw, chop and stack wood that was promptly trucked into the triangle of darkness. Grand Forks, a small town in the British Columbia interior, flew in dozens of high school students from Saint-Jean-sur-Richelieu and McMasterville in what it called "Project Freeze Lift."

Hearts were touched outside Canada, too. In this age of instant communication, news of the ice storm quickly reached the village of Sanankoroba in the West African nation of Mali. For the past 13 years, the 4,500 people of Sanankoroba have been twinned with the 1,500 people of Sainte-Elisabeth, not far from Joliette in rural Quebec, northeast of Montreal. The twinning began with an exchange of dairy farmers and has carried on thanks to work by SUCO, a Quebec aid agency. Mali happens to be one of the poorest countries in the world: on the United Nations scale of development, it ranks right down there with Rwanda and Sierra Leone. But generosity is not a prerogative of the rich.

When the people of Sanankoroba learned about the disaster in Quebec, they got together and collected about $100 – enough to feed a local family for months. They sent the money to Sainte-Elisabeth to help with the relief effort. "Don't think of it as a donation from poor people to rich people," said Moussa Konate, a local teacher. "It's from human beings to other human beings. We think it shows the world that solidarity is not a one-way street."

Sometimes the ice storm brought out the kindness of strangers; other times it revealed the charity of friends. By all accounts, Marguerite Lacroix survived the ice storm with enviable serenity. She's a widow of 79 who lives by herself in the Rosemont district of east-end Montreal; she's also the mother of 21 children. Rosemont was lucky; though its trees were badly damaged, the neighbourhood scarcely lost power. Mme. Lacroix made use of her good fortune: she took in her daughter Hélène, her

Marguerite Lacroix, a 79-year-old widow living in the Rosemont district in Montreal, opened her door to five of her 21 children and their families during the blackout. (Pierre Côté, La Presse)

daughter Thérèse, her daughter Julie, her son Ronald and his girlfriend, and her son Daniel and his family. Other children kept phoning to check up on her and give their advice. She gave them her advice, too.

Mme. Lacroix was perhaps an exception. Most people living under makeshift arrangements found their tempers growing edgy. Kindness was put to the test. Take the case of a Montreal man, a divorced parent who normally shares a home with his two children. After the ice storm tore through Montreal, he opened his doors to others. Within a few days, he and his children were living with his girlfriend, his girlfriend's daughter, his girlfriend's dog, his girlfriend's mother, his girlfriend's mother's

All across Quebec, this was a familiar scene as people without power sought shelter at the homes of their more fortunate relatives outside the storm area. In this Trois-Rivières home, little Alex Bureau, son of former Canadiens player Marc Bureau, seems to be cheering on his dad during a Canadiens game at Tampa. He and his mother, Louise Binette, left their Longueuil home during the blackout to stay with her relatives. Shown here from left to right are Alex, his grandfather Roch Binette, uncle Jean Binette, friend Annie Hébert, grandmother Irène Binette and Louise. (Marie Duhaime, Le Nouvelliste)

Left: It was an emotional time for many. The blackout forced thousands of people out of their homes to look for shelter elsewhere. In Quebec, 454 shelters were set up in community centres, schools, hospitals and arenas. In Ontario, 85 shelters were established to help storm victims. In this photo, seven-year-old Dool Nath cries while sitting on an army bunk at the Little Burgundy shelter in Montreal. (Pierre Obendrauf, The Gazette)

dog, and his ex-wife's dog. One of the dogs (Psycho by name) is deaf. No wonder the man soon began to look somewhat frazzled.

But not everyone and his dog had bright homes to descend upon. Tens of thousands of people spent at least part of the crisis in community shelters. All over the wounded area, they were set up within days of the first freezing rain, often with the help of the Canadian Red Cross. Not quite hotels, not quite hospitals, not quite minimum-security prisons, the shelters were closest in nature to refugee camps. Walk into many of the shelters, and you'd find a wide cross-section of society – young and old, French- and English-speaking, poor and well-to-do, united only by their common plight, a sudden homelessness. Jacob, the New Year's baby for Saint-Jean-sur-Richelieu, moved to a shelter less than a week after his birth; in the same building were people in their 90s.

It's easy to look back on the whole experience through rose-coloured glasses; easy to recall the warmth and the kindness, the laughs and the jokes, that so many people in the shelters shared. It's tempting to forget that homelessness, even on a temporary basis, is nerve-racking. But in truth, time in the shelters tended to pass slowly. Boredom was rife. Television shows seemed more than usually unreal; even so, TV was useful as a weapon of mass distraction. At night, sleep could be difficult. The snores and moans, the prayers, the juvenile giggles, the bitter complaints: to all of these, add the occasional, unpredictable yells and screams. In one shelter, an old woman shouted "Lorraine! Lorraine!" all night long. But no Lorraine appeared. A friend of mine got up in the night to visit the toilet, and almost crushed a sleeping child who had rolled off his mat onto the bare floor.

Shelter refugees, just like hospital patients, often found mealtimes the highlight of the day. The quality of the food varied. Some shelters made a special effort to provide their residents with a varied, even surprising, choice; in others, the fare was nourishing but all too predictable. No one

Léonine François was feeling the strain at the Pierrefonds Arena shelter in suburban Montreal.
(Dave Sidaway, The Gazette)

went to the shelters, of course, in quest of gourmet food. People wanted security, warmth, light. Yet the shelters, too, were at risk of losing power. When the electricity died in a windowless Notre-Dame-de-Grâce shelter that normally functions as a school gym, the pitch-black emptiness was terrifying, and not just to the small children whose families had taken refuge there.

The bewildered, the very old, the very young and their parents: these people had the hardest time of it. Except, of course, for people who trustingly arrived in a shelter and were robbed. The Palais des Congrès – Montreal's convention centre, on the fringe of downtown – witnessed a rash of thefts, a heap of drug abuse and more than one anxiety attack. In Polyvalente Armand-Racicot, the big high school that served as a shelter in Saint-Jean-sur-Richelieu, more than 2,000 victims of the storm dined on cold sandwiches and passed cold nights on cold mattresses. Without hot water, the conditions were barely tolerable. What was intolerable was the handful of teenagers ("little killers, real bandits," the town's mayor called them) who terrorized other people in the shelter until they were finally expelled.

Some cities tried to segregate the old and the young. In Saint-Hyacinthe, another corner of the triangle of darkness, 400 elderly refugees were taken away to a big geriatric hospital. Confused and traumatized by the experience, or stricken by a flu epidemic that raged through the overcrowded wards, some of them never went home.

The best shelters tended to be the ones with the best helpers, the most volunteers. And the volunteers, many of them young people, often were helped and entertained in their own right. An 80-year-old veteran named Robert Hogg moved out of his Kingston apartment after several days in the cold. He ended up at a shelter run by the local psychiatric hospital, where he spent hours regaling Queen's University students with tales of his experiences sailing the North Atlantic with the Royal Canadian Navy.

After two weeks in the shelter at the Polyvalente P-G Ostiguy, a high school in Saint-Césaire, this little girl was ready to go home. Saint-Césaire was blacked out for another two weeks after this photo was taken. (Alain Dion, La Voix de l'Est)

True, he'd seen a smattering of icebergs along the way; but the ships, like a heart, carried on. The Kingston shelter reminded Hogg of shelters he'd seen during the war. And in fact, thousands of Canadians were by then sleeping on U.S. military cots, courtesy of a fast deal that Emergency Preparedness Canada had struck with the Pentagon. The military cots proved more comfortable than the plastic exercise mats that had served as beds when many shelters opened.

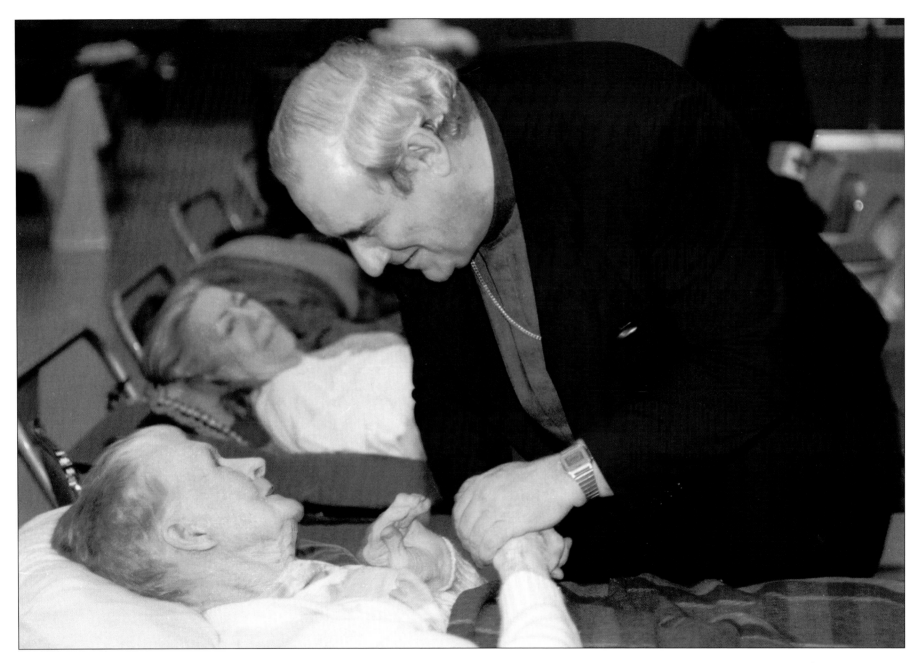

Cardinal Jean-Claude Turcotte tried to reassure people in the Palais des Congrès shelter in Montreal. Ellen McCaw, 83, was one of many elderly people forced to leave their Notre-Dame-de-Grâce homes after the power went out. Parts of the city were without power for almost two weeks. (Robert Skinner, La Presse)

In most of the shelters – along with the hardships, the anxiety and the ennui – an indelible feeling of solidarity set in. This unknown man clutching a lunch tray or tossing on the cot beside you: he was, after all, in your community; a piece of the continent, a part of the main. In the large shelter that the Montreal suburb of Pointe Claire created in its well-known aquatic centre – the pools, unfortunately, had to be kept shut – one tiny, elderly lady was so thrilled by the whole experience, so elated to have company, that she didn't want to go home.

Above: Evelyn Boal, 80, contemplates lunch at the Kemptville, Ontario, storm centre. She is on oxygen and was brought to the shelter when her apartment building was blacked out. (Lynn Ball, Ottawa Citizen).

Left: Anne Picard, a nurses' aide, gets a flu shot from Cpl. Sylvie Paquet at the Saint-Hyacinthe hospital. After being hit by the storm and the blackout, the region suffered a flu outbreak. (Ryan Remiorz, Canadian Press)

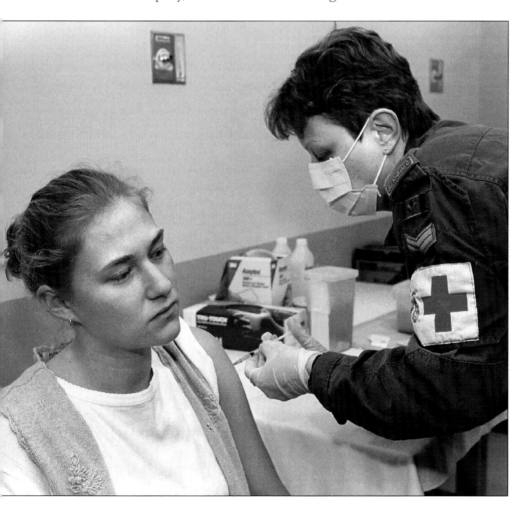

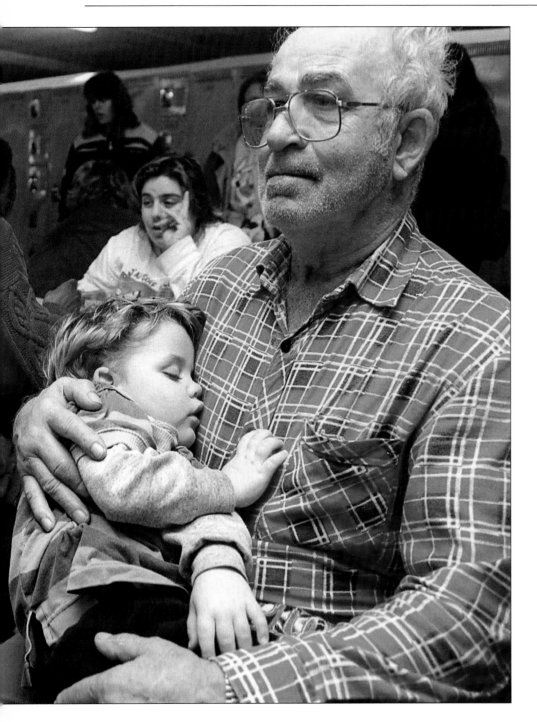

Above: People pulled together during the storm. In the shelters, while there was tension, there was also a deep sense of community. When the power went back on in Greenfield Park on the south shore of Montreal after more than a week, people who had taken refuge in the shelter at Centennial High School wanted to say "Thanks." This message was on the guest sign-out sheet.
(Gordon Beck, The Gazette)

Left: Odile Chouinard holds his three-year-old grandson, Kevin Chouinard, at the Polyvalente Armand-Racicot, a high school in Saint-Jean-sur-Richelieu.
(Gordon Beck, The Gazette)

Glen Aragon, 4, surveys the scene at a shelter in Little Burgundy in Montreal from his refuge under a cot. (Pierre Obendrauf, The Gazette)

Bill and Phyllis Derry, both in their 80s, were making the best of their stay in the shelter in Kemptville, Ontario. (Lynn Ball, Ottawa Citizen)

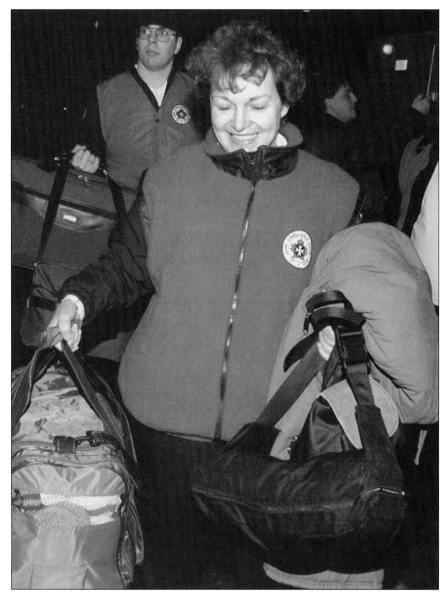

Claude Germain of Saint-Félicien, in the Saguenay region of Quebec, arrives at a suburban bus station in Montreal. She was on her way to the Saint-Jean-sur-Richelieu area to help ice-storm victims. In all, more than 3,300 staff and volunteers helped an estimated 334,000 people affected by the storm.
(Dave Sidaway, The Gazette)

Joe Morena, owner of the famous St. Viateur Bagel Shop in Montreal, fills paper bags with hot bagels that he gave out to customers without power.
(Pierre Obendrauf, The Gazette)

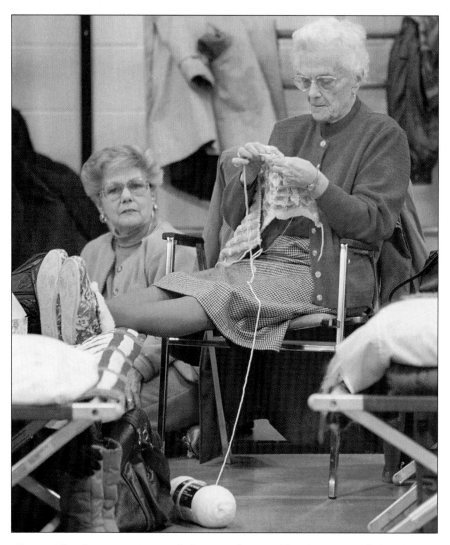

Above: All Lulu Dixon, 85, needed was a chair and her knitting to feel at home at the Recreation Centre shelter in Beaconsfield, Quebec.
(Dave Sidaway, The Gazette)

Left: At the time and later, Ontario Premier Mike Harris toured parts of Ontario hit by the storm and the blackout. Here he poses with five-year-old volunteer Stewart Clelland, one of many volunteers in Maxville and Vankleek Hill. (Julie Oliver, Ottawa Citizen)

Fish-sitting. Aqua Tropical's marine reef and freshwater specialist Shawn Steinberg put a not-for-sale sign on the tank containing a pair of Gold Severum (South American cichlids). Montreal customers brought in their fish for safekeeping during the storm. (Dave Sidaway, The Gazette)

People pitched in whenever they could. A group of Barrhaven, Ontario, boys raised $250 going door to door to buy the ingredients for muffins and cookies at the Barrhaven IGA. The store decided to donate the ingredients, so the boys used the money to buy other foods for people in the shelter at the Stittsville Community Centre. In this photo, they are decorating the cookies with guidance from IGA baker Rick Brazeau in the background. Left to right: Scott Wallace, 12, Tyko Taylor, 11, Nathan Ayer, 12, and Nick Friedrichson, 11. They baked a total of 12 dozen muffins and 40 dozen cookies. (Wayne Hiebert, Ottawa Citizen)

Above: Volunteer Shawn Martel, 11, carries blankets into an emergency shelter in Vankleek Hill, Ontario. (Dave Chan, Ottawa Citizen)

Right: Generators were in demand during the blackout and Richard Rubin of Hampstead, Quebec, with his dog Maggie, were on top of the situation, sharing their power with neighbours. (Gordon Beck, The Gazette)

Chapter Five

MEN OF POWER

"I've worked hurricanes in the States a few times, but it doesn't come close to this. When we arrived, we thought: 'Is this Armageddon?'"

– Harry Morad, line supervisor,
Public Service Electric & Gas Co., Newark, New Jersey

At first this was a weather crisis. But before long, the weather became of small importance. The ice storm paralyzed millions of lives, not because it brought an unheard-of quantity of freezing rain; a 1984 tempest in Newfoundland briefly trapped St. John's in 150 millimetres of ice, more than twice as much as descended on Montreal. Fourteen years later, paralysis set in because the weather succeeded in crippling the power supply to southwestern Quebec, eastern Ontario and northern fragments of New England. Huddling in school gyms, church halls, shopping malls and other shelters, the evacuees didn't pray for a return of fine weather. They prayed for a return of power.

The ice storm demonstrated not that we are prisoners of brutal weather, but that we are all now hostages to electricity. "Plugged in," "high voltage,"

Of all the images of the ice storm, this is one that Quebecers will not soon forget. Premier Lucien Bouchard and Hydro-Quebec president André Caillé, with his signature ice-storm turtleneck sweater, held daily televised news conferences to talk about the need for "solidarity" and keep people up to date on the number of homes blacked out. (Pierre Obendrauf, The Gazette)

Left: Two linemen, precariously perched atop a hydro tower, attempt to reconnect power lines at the Saint-Césaire, Quebec, hydro station. (Dave Sidaway, The Gazette)

"wired," "tuned out": these are more than just figures of speech. They sum up the new fabric of life.

Among the most enduring images of the whole crisis are the fallen pylons, snapped-off poles, contorted wires. In picture after picture, steel rods lie broken like chicken bones across a wilderness of snow: visceral proof that a network had collapsed. It was fun, at first, to improvise: to rig up a propane stove on a driveway, as one of my neighbours did, and cook bacon and eggs outside. It was fun to brew up a pioneer's breakfast in the fireplace, boiling water in a saucepan and using coat-hangers to turn bread into toast. But the fun soon passed. Being trapped in the grid-locked traffic of a pitch-black downtown: that was nerve-racking. Lying awake alone in the dark, wearing a tuque and scarf for warmth, and listening to the wind dismember a tree: that was downright frightening.

Amid chaos, human nature will search for heroes. And the heroes of this crisis surely included the hydro workers – the power rangers, in children's parlance. In Quebec, the best known of them were Denis Bouchard and Jean-Yves Boies, who accomplished a spectacular mission by helicopter on the afternoon of Thursday, January 15. They dangled high above the St. Lawrence River, repairing a line that supplies the island of Montreal with 200 precious megawatts an hour. Hanging off the side of the helicopter in below-zero temperatures and a bruising wind, Bouchard and Boies could be watched live on TV: news as real-life drama, work as entertainment. Down on the ground, the men's supervisor, Alain Trottier, was cursing the cameras; to get the best pictures, a news network had rented a helicopter of its own, one that buzzed dangerously close to the linemen and the iced-up pylon. But Hydro-Quebec was delighted. Not only was Montreal's power supply more secure: so was the reputation of the big utility.

Saint-Isidore on the south shore of Montreal. (Rémi Lemée, La Presse)

In place of the symmetry that pylons normally possess, the ice storm created jagged edges and abrupt curves on a monumental scale. (Martin Chamberland, La Presse)

Hydro-Quebec towers collapsed at Boucherville, Quebec, along Highways 20 and 30. (André Pichette, The Gazette)

Far away from fame, even of the 15-minute variety, thousands of electricity workers in both Quebec and Ontario put in long hours on a job that was often tedious, sometimes dangerous and seldom easy. So did the crews who drove in to help from places like Detroit and Winnipeg, Ohio and New Jersey. When they arrived, aghast at the destruction around them, many of the newcomers needed to be kitted out with long underwear and cotton-lined gloves. Some of the American crews were nervous about working in the dark and on the ice. But they began the task at once, helping rebuild a severely fractured grid. As they did so, these strangers in sunglasses and orange jackets were also reconnecting our collective nervous system.

In the middle of January, a cold snap pushed down from Hudson Bay. Minus 18, minus 20; but the work went on. Whatever errors Ontario Hydro and Hydro-Quebec may have made, the linemen could hardly be faulted. People tried to spur them on by offering them cookies and doughnuts, barbecue-heated coffee, and the unmeasurable gift of applause. "I don't want to go home," a Toronto lineman called Mike Carson told a reporter in Kingston. "When an elderly woman comes up and starts hugging you, that's what keeps you going." Fate was unusually sweet when it flung $1.89 million at seven linemen from Newfoundland, the buyers of a 6-49 lottery ticket during a rare spell of downtime between the raising of new poles near the small Quebec town of Lacolle.

Many of the men spent the better part of three weeks standing in open buckets – "cherry-pickers" in English, "giraffes" in French – suspended high above the frozen ground. They began work in the dark and finished work in the dark. Lunch required a half-hour at most: any longer, and the body's energy would have faded. Typically, a three-man crew can

Right: The road to Marieville, Quebec, January 8. (Armand Trottier, La Presse)

By the end of the storm, 1,000 steel pylons in Quebec and 300 in Ontario had collapsed or been damaged by ice. (Martin Chamberland, La Presse)

hook up eight or ten poles in a day – if the installation is not too complicated. But in some rural districts, more than 80 per cent of all hydro poles needed to be replaced. The progress was agonizingly slow.

Regardless of the weather, nothing quite like this massive breakdown had ever happened in Canada before. Blizzards and ice storms, of course, have taken their toll in the past. Today, just like a generation ago, hospital doctors expect each serious bout of freezing rain to produce a few

broken wrists. The difference now is not in our bodies but our minds. Never have we been so hungry for electricity, so dependent, so unable to withdraw. With our computers and washing machines, our CD players and TV sets, our toaster-ovens and refrigerators, daily life seems hardly imaginable in the absence of electricity. The truth is, we're hooked.

A century ago, farmers and town-dwellers alike were not so vulnerable. They heated by fire. When they had to travel by night, many of them could read the language of stars and planets. Even then, electricity was not exactly new – generators, of a kind, had been known since 1663, when a German physicist named Otto von Guericke attached a sulphur ball to a spindle inside a wooden frame. Yet up to the late nineteenth century, electricity was widely seen as the mere plaything of scientists. It was not until 1892 that some affluent diners at Montreal's Windsor Hotel would consume the first meal in Canada to be cooked entirely by electricity.

Yet ever since the Quiet Revolution of the 1960s, the destinies of Quebec and Hydro-Quebec have been shared and intertwined. More than anywhere else in Canada, Quebec has made its utility not just a public service but a public symbol – which is one reason why the premier, Lucien Bouchard, and the chairman of Hydro-Quebec, André Caillé, seemed almost inseparable in the week or two after the storm. Their joint news conferences became a nightly ritual. The dark-suited politician and the turtlenecked businessman needed each other. Like Winston Churchill during the Battle of Britain, they offered reassurance in a dangerous time. If they didn't stand together, they might have fallen separately. Most Quebecers seemed determined to believe them. The hard questions could wait until later.

Right: Trees, hydro lines, telephone poles – everything came crashing down around Rougemont, Quebec. By Friday, January 9, the ice had caused many of the hydro and telephone lines to collapse. (Denis Courville, La Presse)

Quebec Premier Lucien Bouchard closes his helicopter window after picking up cheques in Sainte-Julie, south of Montreal, to give to ice-storm victims. During times of crisis, leaders must be present at the scene.
(Marcos Townsend, The Gazette)

Eventually, the questions arose. Questions about the collapse of four out of the five links – the "ring of power" – by which Hydro-Quebec feeds the island of Montreal. Questions about why the beloved utility had no contingency plan for working with municipalities, no permanent department for crisis management, not even a computer simulation on how to deal with major power failures. Questions about why, in early January, Hydro-Quebec called in workers from as far away as B.C. and Texas while 4,000 of its own employees were sitting at home on full pay.

In Ontario, too, the masters of power would face probing, uncomfortable queries. While Hydro-Quebec retains a lingering aura of nationalist sanctity, Ontario Hydro enjoys no such exalted status – so it met the hard questions sooner. Why did the utility have no large-scale plan for such an emergency? Why had Ontario Hydro been slow to perform routine maintenance tasks? Could it have responded faster?

During the crisis, electricity became not just a vital commodity (it was already that) but a commodity we thought about. The storm added new words and phrases to our vocabulary. For the first time, many of us became aware of "galloping conductors" – the term that describes what happens when ice-caked power lines start to vibrate amid gusts of wind. The uncontrollable vibrations put added stress on wires and hydro poles, sometimes causing them to topple. Galloping conductors: something else to worry about, for those who were so inclined.

Yet even when electricity was scarce and precious, not everyone bothered to conserve it. A week after the storm began, when downtown Montreal was still supposed to be a ghost town, I happened to walk through a big shopping mall, Les Promenades de la Cathédrale. It contained a boutique with more than a hundred spotlights blazing inside the store. The staff outnumbered the dazzled shoppers. Rock music blared from an oversized speaker. "The decision whether or not to open was left to our discretion," the manager said; then she walked off, refusing to

Hydro pylons soon crumpled under the weight of the ice. (Robert Skinner, La Presse)

Above: Scenes like this one, outside a house in Sainte-Perpétue, were common all across the triangle of darkness. Power in some areas was out for up to 33 days. (Alain Bédard, Le Nouvelliste)

Left: Steve Lusk works on Bell Canada lines coated with ice on Counter Street in Kingston on January 9. (Ian MacAlpine, Kingston Whig-Standard)

Right: Near Saint-Basile-le-Grand, Quebec, two hydro linemen work high above the fields. (Phillip Norton)

answer questions. My dismay began to simmer up into the realm of anger, although the fate of the city would scarcely depend on one boutique's abuse of power.

Now, months later, it's tempting to take electricity for granted once again. We use credit cards and debit cards routinely, forgetting the harsh days when bank machines went dead but cash spoke loud and clear. We sip espressos, mochas and cappuccinos, forgetting the cold hours when a single mug of instant coffee would have tasted like paradise.

No doubt it would be a hard task to recapture that January intimacy with the power that shapes our world. Perhaps only mystics can accomplish it. In a single sheet of paper, a Vietnamese Buddhist teacher named Thich Nhat Hanh once noted, you can see the sun, the clouds, the trees in the forest, even the logger. Inspired by the ice storm, many of us looked a little differently at the quivering wires leading to our homes. So much depended on them! They were surprisingly fragile, surprisingly mortal. In each strand of metal, perhaps, we should still be able to glimpse the northern rainfall and the swirling river, the turbines and transformers of our lives.

Wires snake on the icy ground towards a crumpled pylon, one of 1,300 steel pylons in Quebec and Ontario that collapsed during the ice storm.
(André Pichette, The Gazette)

Eight days after the storm began, ice is still hanging from a church in downtown Saint-Jean-sur-Richelieu, Quebec, and poles are still broken. Power would not be restored to the city for several weeks. (Robert Mailloux, La Presse)

Hydro workers from New Brunswick help establish electricity in Saint-Jean-Baptiste-de-Rouville, Quebec. (Dave Sidaway, The Gazette)

The triangle of darkness.
(André Pichette, The Gazette)

Hydro damage in Saint-Césaire, in the eye of the triangle. (Armand Trottier, La Presse)

Saint-Jean-sur-Richelieu, Quebec, January 8, three days after the storm began. (Armand Trottier, La Presse)

Left: Sunlight over an icy wasteland.
(Phillip Norton)

Right: Toronto hydro workers pitch in to help out in
Ottawa. K-line foreman Ed Spoelstra is shown with
Ottawa Hydro foreman Gary Klein-Swormink (right)
and hydro crew in cherry-pickers.
(Rod MacIvor, Ottawa Citizen)

Crews in cherry-pickers from Connecticut Light and Power repair lines on Irwin Street in Granby. (Alain Dion, La Voix de l'Est)

Above: Bird's-eye view. (Etienne Morin, Le Droit)

Left: Darryl Harrison from Brampton Hydro was on the job repairing hydro lines early enough, Saturday, January 10, to see the sun rise over the St. Lawrence River in Brockville. (Phil Kall, Brockville Recorder and Times)

A Kingston worker clears branches so that felled hydro wires can be replaced. (Michael Lea, Kingston Whig-Standard)

Dave Thiel (left) and Terry Moore, from Waterloo, Ontario, work on a hydro line near the little town of Edwards, Ontario.
(Patrick Doyle, Ottawa Citizen)

Louis Lauzon of the forestry department of Nepean Hydro working on Brenmann Road near Ottawa. (Wayne Hiebert, Ottawa Citizen)

For the people who live on Route 112 in Saint-Paul-d'Abbotsford, Quebec, Milton Hall, a hydro worker with the Detroit Edison company, is a hero. On January 14, temperatures were plunging and Hall braved numbing minus 20C cold to repair the hydro lines. (Alain Dion, La Voix de l'Est)

Above: Storm windfall. For seven linemen from Newfoundland, ice storm '98 was the luckiest disaster ever. The telephone linemen came to Quebec to help Bell Canada repair damage caused by the storm and they each went home more than $250,000 richer. The men had been working in the Sainte-Polycarpe and Lacolle areas near the American border and, after raising some poles, bought three Lotto 6-49 tickets. In the foreground, Roland Taylor (left), Christopher Slade, Kent Samson and Gerard Collier. Behind them are Lorne Strickland (left), TV host Yves Corbeil and crew escort Marc-André Valiquette (who didn't collect), Christopher Crocker and Boyde Howell. (Loto-Québec)

Left: Flying the flag, workers from Connecticut Light and Power were busy reconnecting power lines on Montreal's Oxford Ave. (Peter Martin, The Gazette)

Above: Hydro heroes (left to right) Gary Klein-Swormink of Ottawa Hydro, and Brad Condon, Jonathan Dale, and Ed Spoelstra from Toronto were happy to see a bit of sun on January 12. (Chris Mikula, Ottawa Citizen)

Below: Cary Hastings (left) and Lairn Allin of Langley Utilities from Bowmanville, on contract to Ontario Hydro.
(Wayne Hiebert, Ottawa Citizen)

Right: A 140-member crew from Manitoba Hydro drove 36 hours from their home province to pitch in after the storm. These men flew the Manitoba flag in Casselman, Ontario, where they were working to restore power.
(Julie Oliver, Ottawa Citizen)

Left: It wasn't all work for the Manitoba Hydro crew in Casselman, Ontario. Joking about how mild it was on January 20, a few crew members stripped to flex some Manitoba muscle. Back row, left to right: Larry Thorkelson, Owen Hagan, Sean Cleff. Front row (l-r) Darryl Rempel and Jeff "Chesty" Johnston.
(Julie Oliver, Ottawa Citizen)

Right: Back to work.
(Julie Oliver, Ottawa Citizen)

Above: Prime Minister Jean Chrétien meets American hydro workers who had come to Quebec. (Alain Dion, La Voix de l'Est)

Right: Rebuilding the hydro lines in Sainte-Julie on the south shore of Montreal. (Robert Nadon, La Presse)

Pole by pole, workers put in shifts of 16 hours and more to reconstruct the entire hydro system in the triangle of darkness. Some areas of Quebec were blacked out in the dead of winter for 33 days.
(Alain Dion, La Voix de l'Est)

Chapter Six

AN ACT OF GOD?

"If there's one thing I've learned over the years, it's that all the biggest problems are caused by Mother Nature."

– René Paquette, Emergency Preparedness Canada

A tree sways in the wind, hunchbacked by its cloak of ice, each limb struggling to bear the unaccustomed weight. Below it, the ground appears to be coated not by snow but by a thick meringue. A wind moans and splutters. Sharply, like a pistol shot from the low clouds, a crack rings out: the breaking of a branch. It tumbles halfway to the frozen ground, dangling uselessly in the air. For a moment, nature seems to hang silent and still. Then the wind returns and, over on the next street, comes the next crack, the next dull thud.

All over the storm zone, people stood on their front porches or by their kitchen windows and looked out on a scene like that. There was something terrifying in the random finality of those cracks: trees could snap at any moment in any direction, answering to no appeal. A young maple fell in my backyard, crashing down onto the birdfeeder and the

Almost from the very start, it was clear we were in for a messy storm. Pedestrians along Edouard Montpetit Boulevard in Montreal on January 6 were forced to find a way around fallen tree branches at McKenna Street. (John Mahoney, The Gazette)

Left: On Thursday, January 8, residents of Brockville awoke to scenes like this one in front of a house on King Street West, just east of Cedar Street. (Phil Kall, Brockville Recorder and Times)

Fallen tree on Island Park Drive in Ottawa. (Rod MacIvor, Ottawa Citizen)

clothesline below – a decade of patient growth, erased by a few days' weather. But we were lucky: the tree missed the house. The squirrels, masters of improvisation, were quick to adapt.

A strange, unearthly beauty lurked in the storm and its aftermath. You could see it in the light of day: residents became tourists in their own neighbourhood, checking sightlines and landmarks, allowing their wondering eyes to roam the devastation, noticing the broken world afresh. But as night fell, the streets emptied. Though its sculptures and collages were unchanged, the ice palace turned into an ice prison. In the tree-encrusted darkness, even the most familiar roads took on an air of menace. A siren wailed in the distance; the heart skipped a beat.

Colour it white: any other shades were trouble. Blue or yellow flashes signalled a short circuit on a live wire. Orange flames might mean nothing more serious than the ignition of dead leaves on a wired tree; you hoped they meant nothing more. A horizontal line of orange signified a police cordon; red, a fire engine. And black? Black was the colour of night.

This chaos, this spectacular breakdown: was it nature's revenge on a society grown brash and wasteful in its careless dominance? Perhaps so. During the ordeal, a Hydro-Quebec official confidently explained that the ice storm was a one-in-10,000-year event. People appeared to believe the man, as though he had the remotest idea what the weather had been like 700 or 7,000 years ago, or what it will be like next January. The alternative – to admit our own hubris, our own uncertainty – is unpleasant for a culture that prides itself on control. Great ships, as we know, can be slow to swerve from danger. But in the words of the splendid American essayist Wendell Berry:

"For a long time now, we have understood ourselves as travelling toward some sort of industrial paradise, some new Eden conceived and

On top of Mount Royal. The structure in the background is a broadcast tower. (André Pichette, The Gazette)

constructed entirely by human ingenuity. And we have thought ourselves free to use and abuse nature in any way that might further this enterprise. Now we face overwhelming evidence that we are not smart enough to recover Eden by assault, and that nature does not tolerate or excuse our abuses."

Born of a disruption of the jetstream, the ice storm may ultimately have been a result of El Niño – that strange misbehaviour of ocean currents which once seemed nothing more than a rare curiosity, irrelevant to most of our lives. But even if El Niño was to blame, it doesn't let us off the hook. The growing frequency and intensity of El Niño events in the Pacific are, in all likelihood, intimately linked to global warming. For what is El Niño, if not a way for the tropical regions of the Earth to release a buildup of heat by bringing it to the ocean's surface?

Which means, in turn, that the ice storm – the days when a few million people struggled not to freeze in the dark – can be thought of as one of the by-products of global warming. The changes we've been inflicting on the planet's atmosphere have left no climate untouched. True, the models of global warming are still only models. But they are intricate, sophisticated models. And one of the things they predict is an increase in dramatic, violent weather – exactly what many areas of North America have experienced in the 1990s. It's not just North America, either. The people of the Netherlands endured a "flood of the century" in 1993. Two years later, they endured another one.

The computer models suggest that global warming, despite the gentle, calming tone of the phrase, is a recipe for extremism in the sky. We can't speak with total certainty; a few scientists and the odd newspaper editor still resort to the notion of natural variability. They are far outnumbered,

By Friday, January 9, the city of Montreal was coated in ice.
(Robert Skinner, La Presse)

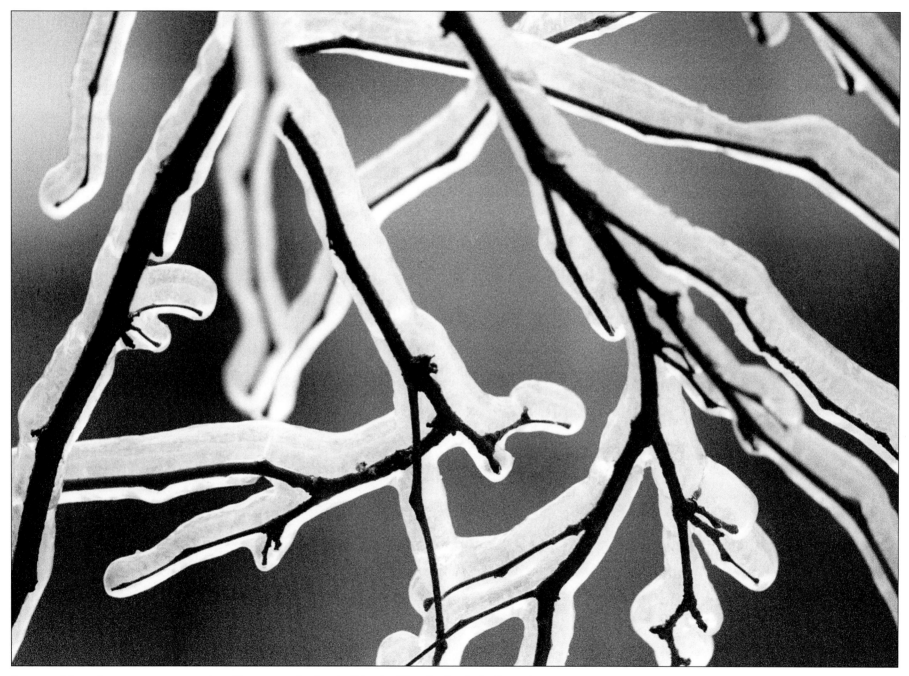

Ice-coated branches trace a strange, river-like pattern in the air. (Martin Chamberland, La Presse)

Headlights and some buildings with generators were the only things lighting up downtown Montreal on Friday evening in this time-exposed photo looking up McGill College Avenue towards McGill University. (Ryan Remiorz, Canadian Press)

however, by those who say that we've already left the realm of "natural" variability behind. Perhaps the ice storm was an act of God. Yet such acts can no longer be ascribed to Him alone.

"Climate will not just change in future; it is doing so today." This was not said by some tub-thumping environmentalist, but by the giant Swiss Re insurance company. In a 1994 report entitled *Global Warming: Element of Risk*, the company admitted that "the danger of unmanageable extreme weather situations is therefore not a future threat but already an acute one."

It took the insurance industry – one of the largest in the world – to sound the alarm bell about climate change. The reason is simple: at its most severe, global warming could bankrupt the industry. The Swiss Re report posits scenarios in which, as a result of disastrous weather events, "the urban system will collapse within days. It is not uncertain that, when major cities are affected, extreme weather situations will cause inconceivably high damage, in the range of one or more per cent of the gross national product, with unmanageable consequences. One possible effect of global climatic change is that cities might have to be abandoned, just as human settlements were in the past. Nobody knows how to cope with such an eventuality."

For the moment, all this belongs to the realm of speculation. But few large cities can ever have come closer to the apocalyptic vision outlined in the Swiss Re report than Montreal did on the afternoon of Friday, January 9 – that wet, stormy day when Hydro-Quebec officials, worried that the whole metropolis could lose power, resorted to deliberate "load-shedding."

The decision meant that within minutes, the city's water-filtration plants and oil refineries were out of action. Though the news was highly sensitive at the time, the electricity network serving the island was as weak as a sick child. In spite of – or because of – the lack of information,

Montrealers, like most Canadians, are used to harsh winters and freezing rain but January's storm was the most damaging in Canadian history. This photo of Park Avenue, taken in 1961, shows some of the damage caused when 30 mm of freezing rain fell over two days. In 1942, 39 mm of freezing rain fell on Montreal over two days. More recently, Ottawa was hit with 30 mm of freezing rain over two days in 1986. In 1984, St. John's, Newfoundland, was hit with 150 mm of freezing rain, far more than what fell on Quebec and Ontario, yet escaped wide-spread damage. (From La Presse files)

rumours spread of a total blackout. Bottled water sold out in dimly lit supermarkets and corner stores. Families abandoned their homes. Gingerly they made for the shelters, clutching garbage bags, pillows and suitcases full of clothes and essential belongings. Yet they couldn't easily leave Montreal. Half the subway system had shut down, and the highways to the suburbs were gridlocked. Bridges on and off the island were closed, in deference to the risk of falling ice. Nearly two million people were trapped, fearing the worst.

The worst never came to pass. The power system did not shut down entirely, nor did any major fires break out. But if conditions had worsened further, and if the bridges had been in working order – if, in short, it had been a simple matter to escape the island of Montreal – a city might have tried to flee.

Left: On Hampton Street in Notre-Dame-de-Grâce, residents wore hardhats to protect themselves from falling ice and branches as they began to clear debris from the street, their driveways and their yards.
(Marcos Townsend, The Gazette)

Right: On Friday, four days after the storm began, about 1.4 million homes were blacked out in Quebec and Ontario, affecting an estimated 3.5 million people. By mid-afternoon, much of downtown Montreal had lost its power, including the water-filtration plants. Civil security officials advised people to boil their water, if they could. Half the city's subway stations and east-end oil refineries were also shut down. In this picture, a police cruiser drives on Ste. Catherine Street.
(John Kenney, The Gazette)

A typical Montreal street scene. (André Pichette, The Gazette)

Saint Andrew's United Church in Châteauguay. (Phillip Norton)

The devastating beauty of the ice storm brought out amateur and professional photographers in droves to shoot in the rain. Icy branches, snapped off trees in Dominion Square, caught this Montreal photographer's eye. (Martin Chamberland, La Presse)

Above: Arlène Gaudreault of Montreal is one of the many amateur photographers who spent hours in the rain and cold in awe of what was happening. This photo shows the street outside her house in the Notre-Dame-de-Grâce district on Wednesday, January 7. (Arlène Gaudreault)

Right: Lorna Jessemy poses under an arch of ice-covered branches for a picture by friend Gerald Martin in the early-morning chill along Craig Henry Drive in Nepean, Ontario. (Wayne Cuddington, Ottawa Citizen)

Above: Ice balls on a frozen shrub. (Arlène Gaudreault)

Left: A pine branch. (Arlène Gaudreault)

The beauty of ice-coated fields caught photographer Phillip Norton's artistic eye. This weed was photographed near Saint-Rémi, Quebec. (Phillip Norton)

A fence in Saint-Rémi, Quebec. (Phillip Norton)

In a field, blades of grass collect ice from the freezing rain. (Phillip Norton)

Bird house in Châteauguay, Quebec. (Phillip Norton)

*Ice couldn't hurt this inukshuk outside The Museum
of Civilization in Hull, Quebec.*
(Lynn Ball, Ottawa Citizen)

The top of Mount Royal resembled a broken wilderness. (André Pichette, The Gazette)

Ten days after the freezing rain began, the ice was still thick on these lawn ornaments outside a home on Highway 227 near Rougemont, Quebec.
(Peter Martin, The Gazette)

Chapter Seven

OUTLASTING THE ICE

"Then the Lord answered Job out of the whirlwind and said . . . Hast thou entered into the treasures of the snow? . . . Out of whose womb came the ice?"
— Job 38: 1, 22, 29

We endured. We made it through. It wasn't easy; it wasn't pretty. When the storm ceased to be spectacular and the hardships began to look merely repetitive or routine, Peter Mansbridge and Lloyd Robertson took off their parkas and flew back to the studios in Toronto. Bernard Derome went back inside. Local newspapers ran dutiful pictures of politicians making sympathy visits by helicopter: Jean Chrétien to Wolfe Island, Lucien Bouchard to Sainte-Julie, Mike Harris to Nepean. Then the politicians, too, headed elsewhere. Fortunately, the hydro crews kept working.

Hour by hour, the pockets of urban darkness dwindled in size. As buildings chilled out, some homeowners drained their pipes just in time. Others left it too late, and spent the following weeks dealing with the mess. Plants and all too many pets had died. Cupboards needed to be restocked, appliances reset. It took weeks or months for city crews to

Left: This family in Rougemont, Quebec, packed up a few belongings and fled their freezing home on Friday, January 9, to seek shelter elsewhere. (Denis Courville, La Presse)

Ten days after the storm began, this farm in Saint-Jean-Baptiste-de-Rouville, Quebec, was still in a deep freeze. (Dave Sidaway, The Gazette)

Farm in Saint-Césaire, Quebec. (Robert Skinner, La Presse)

clear the mangled trees off sidestreets, days to reopen offices and schools. But for the most part, the cities saw normality, or a rough fac-simile, return with surprising speed. The national media, relentlessly moving on, turned the brunt of their attention to catchier topics – Bill Clinton and Monica Lewinsky, for example.

Yet away from the TV cameras, in the darkened solitude of homes and the enforced camaraderie of shelters, people were still living without power. In dozens of towns and villages, and on thousands of farms, peo-ple were still living without power. In Quebec's triangle of darkness and the southeast corner of Ontario, most people were still living without power. Those were the areas where the power lines had suffered such tremendous damage that repairing made less sense than rebuilding.

Feeling that the media had forgotten or overlooked their plight, some people in outlying areas were irked by the declining coverage. Rightly or wrongly, attention seemed proof of care. Mike Metcalfe, a resident of Long Sault, near Cornwall, wrote a fierce letter of complaint: "Cornwall and its satellite communities . . . as well as myriad hamlets and rural routes have been lost in the shuffle. It's beginning to get under our skin. While we can, with considerable tolerance I might add, overlook the fact that we are generally ignored by the Ottawa media at the best of times, this is a tad different."

Because the ordeal in rural areas lasted so long after power was flow-ing again to the cities, the early solidarity among crisis victims dissolved. Patience wore thin. Divisions emerged: not, for the most part, along the old linguistic or political lines, but between those with power and those without. Most of the have-nots were living east and south of Montreal. They were the people unquestionably eligible for the Quebec govern-ment's controversial $10-a-day compensation plan – what critics quickly

A farmer's fence near Cantley, Quebec. (Drew Gragg, Ottawa Citizen)

labelled "Bouchard bucks." By January 21, there were only 75 homes and businesses left to reconnect in Montreal, less than 2,400 in the Laurentians and Gatineau area of Quebec, and about 17,500 in Ontario. But in the region of Quebec that encompassed the triangle of darkness, 166,200 homes and businesses remained in the dark.

January crept away. February slouched in. Even then, more than 60,000 people – almost all of them in the region that French-language media called the "infernal triangle" – continued to wait for heat, light, work, diversion, everything that is bound up in the idea of "normal life." The novelty had ended for them, the excitement was over, but the whole experience dragged on. Never have children seemed so eager to get back to school.

No longer did the evacuees, or those still toughing it out with fire-places and generators at home, feel that we were all in it together; we weren't, not any more. "We" had become a delicate word, a term requiring careful use. In the worst-afflicted areas, the resilience shown by people of all ages was little short of remarkable. But it took a toll. It left scars.

Not until February 8 – a full five weeks after the storm hit – did Hydro-Quebec restore electricity to the homes of the final hundred customers in the triangle of darkness. (On the far side of the planet, the Sumo wrestlers had performed their ritual blessing and the Nagano Olympics were underway.) It would take even longer before all the sugar shacks, irrigation lines and winter chalets of southern Quebec were reconnected. The physical impact of the ice storm, especially in tree-battered parks like Mount Royal, will be felt for years to come. The psychological impact, too.

"Without question," wrote David Phillips in his recent book *Blame It on the Weather*, "the storm directly affected more people than any previous weather event in Canadian history. . . . What it took human beings a half century to construct took nature a matter of hours to knock down." And what kept us going through the crisis? Not just reserves of food and goodwill; not just the devotion of Hydro crews, soldiers and Red Cross officials; not just the literal hope of a brighter tomorrow. What kept us going were stories.

Newspapers throughout the affected area performed heroic feats to get the printed word and much-needed information to an anxious public. Equally important was the work of many radio stations. For the ice storm, like the world war of a previous generation, proved the power of radio. Crouched by a transistor, you could hear advice on how to kindle light and heat by soaking a kitchen rag in a bowl of vegetable oil. You

Near Saint-Jean-Baptiste-de-Rouville, January 15. (Dave Sidaway, The Gazette)

Above: There was nothing to fear from these hydro wires strewn across the road in Saint-Isidore, Quebec. They would be dead for weeks. (Phillip Norton)

Right: Hydro under ice. (Rémi Lemée, La Presse)

could hear up-to-the-minute news about shelters and emergency aid. You could hear stern warnings about what not to do: heat your home with a barbecue, for example. You could phone in for suggestions about keeping an iguana warm; and, if you were the listener to CFJR in Brockville who did exactly that, you (or your reptile) could benefit from four or five replies.

Most of all, you could hear other people telling their tales and pouring out their feelings. Radio can be the most democratic of media. It allows everyone to tell their story, rich or poor, old or young, ugly or beautiful. During the ice storm, I listened avidly to open-line radio shows: there were things I might need to know; and perhaps Mme. Fortier from Saint-Hyacinthe, or Mr. MacKenzie from Hudson Heights, would have the answer. Even if they didn't, there was a kind of reassurance in hearing them speak. Misery loves company. Listening to other people describe their own ways of coping, we seemed less vulnerable ourselves. We were not, after all, alone.

Powerlessness, it became clear, was not just a function of age or poverty or physical isolation. The most powerless, in a sense, were those who lacked not only heat and light, but also a radio with usable batteries. Such people were alone with their thoughts. They had no one to hear their stories, and no one else's stories to share.

The crisis reminded us of who our neighbours really are: not some disembodied voice pouring out words in cyberspace, but the flesh-and-blood people who dwell in nearby homes. In a recent book called *The Virtual Community*, Howard Rheingold boasted about the emergence of a "global nervous system" and an "organic neural network."

Ontario Hydro towers collapsed in a frozen field near Russell, Ontario. Damage to Ontario Hydro's system was severe, although less so than in Quebec. More than 11,000 poles, 1,000 transformers and 300 steel towers were damaged in Ontario. (Lynn Ball, Ottawa Citizen)

But under the pressure of ice, the "virtual community" virtually dissolved. E-mail acquaintances didn't open up their homes for us; e-mail acquaintances were devoid of wood, generators and local gossip. E-mail acquaintances could do no more than cheer or gripe from the organic neural sidelines.

What re-established neighbourliness, then, was a massive failure of electrical technology. Deprived of our usual gadgets, we were free to make contact with our community – to be, if you like, interactive. But it's not quite so simple as that. Radio, too, is a product of technical ingenuity. And radio helped bring people together.

In Ang Lee's brilliant movie *The Ice Storm*, deteriorating weather becomes a symbol of the moral paralysis of America in the early 1970s. The action takes place at Thanksgiving, yet the film's bewildered characters have no idea what to be thankful for. Long before the lethal rain falls from the sky, they already live with chunks of ice embedded in their hearts. Human warmth has gone into the deep freeze. But that was fiction. In the realm of fact, the storm of 1998 brought out a tremendous generosity. To speak of human emotion, the storm generated untold warmth.

No need to be sentimental: the crisis also generated a certain amount of price gouging and theft. Months later, it also proved to have generated serious mistrust – of institutions, not of individuals. Springtime hearings set up by the Quebec government in the wake of the crisis revealed a depth of lingering anger about the way the emergency had been handled. Municipal politicians attacked the civil protection agency; the public security department criticized the local politicians; Hydro-Quebec came under frequent fire. If – when – another major crisis occurs, the preparation and coordination need to be much improved.

Jeannette Wilson listens for news on her mattress at the shelter in the Sacré Coeur high school in Granby, Quebec. (Pierre McCann, La Presse)

CLAUDE JODOIN
ferme
végétale
S.C.A. DE ST-DAMASE

On a wider level, the crisis forced many of us to wonder about the security of our way of life. Our vulnerability to the furies has turned out to be much greater than anyone had imagined. But perhaps "full protection" is a misnomer, a contradiction in terms. In the new science of chaos theory, a key insight or metaphor is that the beating of a butterfly's wings somewhere in Brazil could ultimately set off a tornado in Texas. It's a planner's nightmare, an anarchist's delight. For as I.G. Simmons observed in his recent book *Changing the Face of the Earth*, "What history and chaos theory together seem to indicate is that no system is safe from unpredictable change." We can't predict what the next emergency will be. Yet we can surely be better prepared to meet it.

Even in the triangle of darkness, power eventually came back. The shelters in Granby, Saint-Jean-sur-Richelieu and Saint-Hyacinthe closed down; the grimy, exhausted residents went home. No longer would they have to pass their days watching interminable soap operas and playing endless games of cribbage and bingo; no longer would they have to spend their nights listening to the snoring of strangers. Before the last of them were back in their freezing apartments and houses, local cinemas reopened their doors. *Titanic*, not surprisingly, did roaring business once again. When they wanted a break from the complex chores of re-establishing a home, people from across the afflicted region drove to see it.

But now, as the warm travellers huddled in their seats, munching popcorn and watching a supposedly invulnerable machine lurch unprepared into history, the tale seemed freshly apt. They had made it to the lifeboats, these watchers in the cinema; they had suffered through a long darkness; they had outfaced the ice; they had survived.

With a ledge of solid ice hanging ominously overhead, a farmer in Saint-Jean-Baptiste-de-Rouville climbs up to knock the ice off his barn roof.
(Dave Sidaway, The Gazette)

Above: An ice-covered truck near Chambly, Quebec.
(Peter Martin, The Gazette)

Right: This wagon on a farm in Quebec looks frozen in time.
(Dave Sidaway, The Gazette)

Breaking up the ice on the Richelieu River. (Marcos Townsend, The Gazette)

Sylvia Powell and her dog Djukei play with a stick in Montreal's Lafontaine Park. Behind them are tall piles of wood chips ground up from the trees and branches brought down by the ice storm. (Gordon Beck, The Gazette)

Many people were reluctant to leave their homes. Gerald Myles, 80, sits by a candle in his blacked-out home in Ramsay Township, Ontario.
(Bruno Schlumberger, Ottawa Citizen)

Above: Workers clear snow along Highway 30 to replace downed hydro lines..
(Dave Sidaway, The Gazette)

Right: The ice was impartial: it trapped machines and trees alike.
(Drew Gragg, Ottawa Citizen)

Left: Régis Tremblay and his colleagues work on lines damaged by the ice storm in south shore Saint-Mathias, Quebec. Tremblay averaged 16-hour days while repairing the storm's damage. (Marcos Townsend, The Gazette)

Right: Resigned to a long wait for clean-up crews or a spring thaw, a stone angel in Notre-Dame-des-Neiges Cemetery on Mount Royal ponders the aftermath of the ice storm. (Gordon Beck, The Gazette)

Contributing Photographers

Richard Arless,
The Gazette

Lynn Ball,
Ottawa Citizen

Gordon Beck,
The Gazette

Alain Bédard,
Le Nouvelliste

Bernard Brault,
La Presse

Mark Calder,
Brockville Recorder and Times

Phil Carpenter,
The Gazette

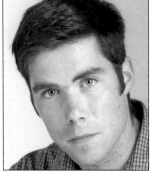

Martin Chamberland,
La Presse

Dave Chan,
Ottawa Citizen

Paul Chiasson,
Canadian Press

Deanna Clark,
Brockville Recorder and Times

Marie-France Coallier,
The Gazette

Peter Cooney,
The Gazette

Pierre Côté,
La Presse

Denis Courville,
La Presse

Wayne Cuddington,
Ottawa Citizen

Alain Dion,
La Voix de l'Est

Patrick Doyle,
Ottawa Citizen

Marie Duhaime,
La Nouvelliste

Belinda Foster,
Cornwall Standard Freeholder

Nick Gardiner,
Brockville Recorder and Times

Jean Goupil,
La Presse

Drew Gragg,
Ottawa Citizen

Wayne Hiebert,
Ottawa Citizen

Phil Kall,
Brockville Recorder and Times

John Kenney,
The Gazette

Michael Lea,
Kingston Whig-Standard

Rémi Lemée,
La Presse

Todd Lihou,
Cornwall Standard Freeholder

Ian MacAlpine,
Kingston Whig-Standard

Rod MacIvor,
Ottawa Citizen

Robert Mailloux,
La Presse

John Mahoney,
The Gazette

John Major,
Ottawa Citizen

Malak,
Ottawa Citizen

Sylvain Marier,
Le Droit

Pierre McCann,
La Presse

Pat McGrath,
Ottawa Citizen

Chris Mikula,
Ottawa Citizen

Etienne Morin,
Le Droit

Dave Mullington,
Ottawa Citizen

Robert Nadon,
La Presse

Philip Norton

Pierre Obendrauf,
The Gazette

Julie Oliver,
Ottawa Citizen

André Pichette,
The Gazette

Ryan Remiorz,
Canadian Press

Michel St-Jean,
La Voix de l'Est

Bruno Schlumberger,
Ottawa Citizen

Dave Sidaway,
The Gazette

Robert Skinner,
La Presse

Marcos Townsend,
The Gazette

Armand Trottier,
La Presse

Ronald Zajac,
Brockville Recorder and Times